ISBN 0-8373-0317-6

C-317     CAREER EXAMINATION SERIES

*This is your*
*PASSBOOK® for...*

# School Lunch Coordinator

*Test Preparation Study Guide*

*Questions & Answers*

**NATIONAL LEARNING CORPORATION**

# PASSBOOK®
## NOTICE

# PASSBOOK® SERIES

THE *PASSBOOK® SERIES* has been created to prepare applicants and candidates for the ultimate academic battlefield – the examination room.

At some time in our lives, each and every one of us may be required to take an examination – for validation, matriculation, admission, qualification, registration, certification, or licensure.

Based on the assumption that every applicant or candidate has met the basic formal educational standards, has taken the required number of courses, and read the necessary texts, the *PASSBOOK® SERIES* furnishes the one special preparation which may assure passing with confidence, instead of failing with insecurity. Examination questions – together with answers – are furnished as the basic vehicle for study so that the mysteries of the examination and its compounding difficulties may be eliminated or diminished by a sure method.

This book is meant to help you pass your examination provided that you qualify and are serious in your objective.

The entire field is reviewed through the huge store of content information which is succinctly presented through a provocative and challenging approach – the question-and-answer method.

A climate of success is established by furnishing the correct answers at the end of each test.

You soon learn to recognize types of questions, forms of questions, and patterns of questioning. You may even begin to anticipate expected outcomes.

You perceive that many questions are repeated or adapted so that you can gain acute insights, which may enable you to score many sure points.

You learn how to confront new questions, or types of questions, and to attack them confidently and work out the correct answers.

You note objectives and emphases, and recognize pitfalls and dangers, so that you may make positive educational adjustments.

Moreover, you are kept fully informed in relation to new concepts, methods, practices, and directions in the field.

You discover that you are actually taking the examination all the time: you are preparing for the examination by "taking" an examination, not by reading extraneous and/or supererogatory textbooks.

In short, this PASSBOOK®, used directedly, should be an important factor in helping you to pass your test.

# SCHOOL LUNCH COORDINATOR

## DUTIES

An employee in this class performs responsible administrative work in reviewing, recommending, and coordinating contractual agreements with private food service companies. The work consists of maintaining financial control, responding to service complaints and insuring the nutritional value of meals served. The work differs from that of the School Lunch Manager position in that the School Lunch Coordinator is not required to exercise supervision over Cooks and Food Service Workers. The work is performed under the general supervision of an assigned school administrator and is reviewed through conferences and written reports. Does related work as required.

## SCOPE OF THE EXAMINATION

The written test will cover knowledge, skills, and/or abilities in such areas as:

1. Overseeing food service operations;
2. Office record keeping;
3. Preparing written material.

# HOW TO TAKE A TEST

## I. YOU MUST PASS AN EXAMINATION

### A. *WHAT EVERY CANDIDATE SHOULD KNOW*

Examination applicants often ask us for help in preparing for the written test. What can I study in advance? What kinds of questions will be asked? How will the test be given? How will the papers be graded?

As an applicant for a civil service examination, you may be wondering about some of these things. Our purpose here is to suggest effective methods of advance study and to describe civil service examinations.

Your chances for success on this examination can be increased if you know how to prepare. Those "pre-examination jitters" can be reduced if you know what to expect. You can even experience an adventure in good citizenship if you know why civil service exams are given.

### B. *WHY ARE CIVIL SERVICE EXAMINATIONS GIVEN?*

Civil service examinations are important to you in two ways. As a citizen, you want public jobs filled by employees who know how to do their work. As a job seeker, you want a fair chance to compete for that job on an equal footing with other candidates. The best-known means of accomplishing this two-fold goal is the competitive examination.

Exams are widely publicized throughout the nation. They may be administered for jobs in federal, state, city, municipal, town or village governments or agencies.

Any citizen may apply, with some limitations, such as the age or residence of applicants. Your experience and education may be reviewed to see whether you meet the requirements for the particular examination. When these requirements exist, they are reasonable and applied consistently to all applicants. Thus, a competitive examination may cause you some uneasiness now, but it is your privilege and safeguard.

### C. *HOW ARE CIVIL SERVICE EXAMS DEVELOPED?*

Examinations are carefully written by trained technicians who are specialists in the field known as "psychological measurement," in consultation with recognized authorities in the field of work that the test will cover. These experts recommend the subject matter areas or skills to be tested; only those knowledges or skills important to your success on the job are included. The most reliable books and source materials available are used as references. Together, the experts and technicians judge the difficulty level of the questions.

Test technicians know how to phrase questions so that the problem is clearly stated. Their ethics do not permit "trick" or "catch" questions. Questions may have been tried out on sample groups, or subjected to statistical analysis, to determine their usefulness.

Written tests are often used in combination with performance tests, ratings of training and experience, and oral interviews. All of these measures combine to form the best-known means of finding the right person for the right job.

## II. HOW TO PASS THE WRITTEN TEST

### A. NATURE OF THE EXAMINATION
To prepare intelligently for civil service examinations, you should know how they differ from school examinations you have taken. In school you were assigned certain definite pages to read or subjects to cover. The examination questions were quite detailed and usually emphasized memory. Civil service exams, on the other hand, try to discover your present ability to perform the duties of a position, plus your potentiality to learn these duties. In other words, a civil service exam attempts to predict how successful you will be. Questions cover such a broad area that they cannot be as minute and detailed as school exam questions.

In the public service similar kinds of work, or positions, are grouped together in one "class." This process is known as *position-classification*. All the positions in a class are paid according to the salary range for that class. One class title covers all of these positions, and they are all tested by the same examination.

### B. FOUR BASIC STEPS

#### 1) Study the announcement
How, then, can you know what subjects to study? Our best answer is: "Learn as much as possible about the class of positions for which you've applied." The exam will test the knowledge, skills and abilities needed to do the work.

Your most valuable source of information about the position you want is the official exam announcement. This announcement lists the training and experience qualifications. Check these standards and apply only if you come reasonably close to meeting them.

The brief description of the position in the examination announcement offers some clues to the subjects which will be tested. Think about the job itself. Review the duties in your mind. Can you perform them, or are there some in which you are rusty? Fill in the blank spots in your preparation.

Many jurisdictions preview the written test in the exam announcement by including a section called "Knowledge and Abilities Required," "Scope of the Examination," or some similar heading. Here you will find out specifically what fields will be tested.

#### 2) Review your own background
Once you learn in general what the position is all about, and what you need to know to do the work, ask yourself which subjects you already know fairly well and which need improvement. You may wonder whether to concentrate on improving your strong areas or on building some background in your fields of weakness. When the announcement has specified "some knowledge" or "considerable knowledge," or has used adjectives like "beginning principles of..." or "advanced ... methods," you can get a clue as to the number and difficulty of questions to be asked in any given field. More questions, and hence broader coverage, would be included for those subjects which are more important in the work. Now weigh your strengths and weaknesses against the job requirements and prepare accordingly.

#### 3) Determine the level of the position
Another way to tell how intensively you should prepare is to understand the level of the job for which you are applying. Is it the entering level? In other words, is this the position in which beginners in a field of work are hired? Or is it an intermediate or advanced level? Sometimes this is indicated by such words as "Junior" or "Senior" in the class title. Other jurisdictions use Roman numerals to designate the level – Clerk I, Clerk II, for example. The word "Supervisor" sometimes appears in the title. If the level is not indicated by the title,

check the description of duties. Will you be working under very close supervision, or will you have responsibility for independent decisions in this work?

## 4) Choose appropriate study materials

Now that you know the subjects to be examined and the relative amount of each subject to be covered, you can choose suitable study materials. For beginning level jobs, or even advanced ones, if you have a pronounced weakness in some aspect of your training, read a modern, standard textbook in that field. Be sure it is up to date and has general coverage. Such books are normally available at your library, and the librarian will be glad to help you locate one. For entry-level positions, questions of appropriate difficulty are chosen – neither highly advanced questions, nor those too simple. Such questions require careful thought but not advanced training.

If the position for which you are applying is technical or advanced, you will read more advanced, specialized material. If you are already familiar with the basic principles of your field, elementary textbooks would waste your time. Concentrate on advanced textbooks and technical periodicals. Think through the concepts and review difficult problems in your field.

These are all general sources. You can get more ideas on your own initiative, following these leads. For example, training manuals and publications of the government agency which employs workers in your field can be useful, particularly for technical and professional positions. A letter or visit to the government department involved may result in more specific study suggestions, and certainly will provide you with a more definite idea of the exact nature of the position you are seeking.


## III. KINDS OF TESTS

Tests are used for purposes other than measuring knowledge and ability to perform specified duties. For some positions, it is equally important to test ability to make adjustments to new situations or to profit from training. In others, basic mental abilities not dependent on information are essential. Questions which test these things may not appear as pertinent to the duties of the position as those which test for knowledge and information. Yet they are often highly important parts of a fair examination. For very general questions, it is almost impossible to help you direct your study efforts. What we can do is to point out some of the more common of these general abilities needed in public service positions and describe some typical questions.

### 1) General information

Broad, general information has been found useful for predicting job success in some kinds of work. This is tested in a variety of ways, from vocabulary lists to questions about current events. Basic background in some field of work, such as sociology or economics, may be sampled in a group of questions. Often these are principles which have become familiar to most persons through exposure rather than through formal training. It is difficult to advise you how to study for these questions; being alert to the world around you is our best suggestion.

### 2) Verbal ability

An example of an ability needed in many positions is verbal or language ability. Verbal ability is, in brief, the ability to use and understand words. Vocabulary and grammar tests are typical measures of this ability. Reading comprehension or paragraph interpretation questions are common in many kinds of civil service tests. You are given a paragraph of written material and asked to find its central meaning.

## 3) Numerical ability

Number skills can be tested by the familiar arithmetic problem, by checking paired lists of numbers to see which are alike and which are different, or by interpreting charts and graphs. In the latter test, a graph may be printed in the test booklet which you are asked to use as the basis for answering questions.

## 4) Observation

A popular test for law-enforcement positions is the observation test. A picture is shown to you for several minutes, then taken away. Questions about the picture test your ability to observe both details and larger elements.

## 5) Following directions

In many positions in the public service, the employee must be able to carry out written instructions dependably and accurately. You may be given a chart with several columns, each column listing a variety of information. The questions require you to carry out directions involving the information given in the chart.

## 6) Skills and aptitudes

Performance tests effectively measure some manual skills and aptitudes. When the skill is one in which you are trained, such as typing or shorthand, you can practice. These tests are often very much like those given in business school or high school courses. For many of the other skills and aptitudes, however, no short-time preparation can be made. Skills and abilities natural to you or that you have developed throughout your lifetime are being tested.

Many of the general questions just described provide all the data needed to answer the questions and ask you to use your reasoning ability to find the answers. Your best preparation for these tests, as well as for tests of facts and ideas, is to be at your physical and mental best. You, no doubt, have your own methods of getting into an exam-taking mood and keeping "in shape." The next section lists some ideas on this subject.

## IV. KINDS OF QUESTIONS

Only rarely is the "essay" question, which you answer in narrative form, used in civil service tests. Civil service tests are usually of the short-answer type. Full instructions for answering these questions will be given to you at the examination. But in case this is your first experience with short-answer questions and separate answer sheets, here is what you need to know:

### 1) Multiple-choice Questions

Most popular of the short-answer questions is the "multiple choice" or "best answer" question. It can be used, for example, to test for factual knowledge, ability to solve problems or judgment in meeting situations found at work.

A multiple-choice question is normally one of three types—
- It can begin with an incomplete statement followed by several possible endings. You are to find the one ending which *best* completes the statement, although some of the others may not be entirely wrong.
- It can also be a complete statement in the form of a question which is answered by choosing one of the statements listed.

- It can be in the form of a problem – again you select the best answer.

Here is an example of a multiple-choice question with a discussion which should give you some clues as to the method for choosing the right answer:

When an employee has a complaint about his assignment, the action which will *best* help him overcome his difficulty is to
  A. discuss his difficulty with his coworkers
  B. take the problem to the head of the organization
  C. take the problem to the person who gave him the assignment
  D. say nothing to anyone about his complaint

In answering this question, you should study each of the choices to find which is best. Consider choice "A" – Certainly an employee may discuss his complaint with fellow employees, but no change or improvement can result, and the complaint remains unresolved. Choice "B" is a poor choice since the head of the organization probably does not know what assignment you have been given, and taking your problem to him is known as "going over the head" of the supervisor. The supervisor, or person who made the assignment, is the person who can clarify it or correct any injustice. Choice "C" is, therefore, correct. To say nothing, as in choice "D," is unwise. Supervisors have and interest in knowing the problems employees are facing, and the employee is seeking a solution to his problem.

## 2) True/False Questions

The "true/false" or "right/wrong" form of question is sometimes used. Here a complete statement is given. Your job is to decide whether the statement is right or wrong.

SAMPLE: A roaming cell-phone call to a nearby city costs less than a non-roaming call to a distant city.

This statement is wrong, or false, since roaming calls are more expensive.

This is not a complete list of all possible question forms, although most of the others are variations of these common types. You will always get complete directions for answering questions. Be sure you understand *how* to mark your answers – ask questions until you do.


## V. RECORDING YOUR ANSWERS

Computer terminals are used more and more today for many different kinds of exams.

For an examination with very few applicants, you may be told to record your answers in the test booklet itself. Separate answer sheets are much more common. If this separate answer sheet is to be scored by machine – and this is often the case – it is highly important that you mark your answers correctly in order to get credit.

An electronic scoring machine is often used in civil service offices because of the speed with which papers can be scored. Machine-scored answer sheets must be marked with a pencil, which will be given to you. This pencil has a high graphite content which responds to the electronic scoring machine. As a matter of fact, stray dots may register as answers, so do not let your pencil rest on the answer sheet while you are pondering the correct answer. Also, if your pencil lead breaks or is otherwise defective, ask for another.

Since the answer sheet will be dropped in a slot in the scoring machine, be careful not to bend the corners or get the paper crumpled.

The answer sheet normally has five vertical columns of numbers, with 30 numbers to a column. These numbers correspond to the question numbers in your test booklet. After each number, going across the page are four or five pairs of dotted lines. These short dotted lines have small letters or numbers above them. The first two pairs may also have a "T" or "F" above the letters. This indicates that the first two pairs only are to be used if the questions are of the true-false type. If the questions are multiple choice, disregard the "T" and "F" and pay attention only to the small letters or numbers.

Answer your questions in the manner of the sample that follows:

32. The largest city in the United States is
   A. Washington, D.C.
   B. New York City
   C. Chicago
   D. Detroit
   E. San Francisco

1) Choose the answer you think is best. (New York City is the largest, so "B" is correct.)
2) Find the row of dotted lines numbered the same as the question you are answering. (Find row number 32)
3) Find the pair of dotted lines corresponding to the answer. (Find the pair of lines under the mark "B.")
4) Make a solid black mark between the dotted lines.

## VI. BEFORE THE TEST

Common sense will help you find procedures to follow to get ready for an examination. Too many of us, however, overlook these sensible measures. Indeed, nervousness and fatigue have been found to be the most serious reasons why applicants fail to do their best on civil service tests. Here is a list of reminders:

- Begin your preparation early – Don't wait until the last minute to go scurrying around for books and materials or to find out what the position is all about.
- Prepare continuously – An hour a night for a week is better than an all-night cram session. This has been definitely established. What is more, a night a week for a month will return better dividends than crowding your study into a shorter period of time.
- Locate the place of the exam – You have been sent a notice telling you when and where to report for the examination. If the location is in a different town or otherwise unfamiliar to you, it would be well to inquire the best route and learn something about the building.
- Relax the night before the test – Allow your mind to rest. Do not study at all that night. Plan some mild recreation or diversion; then go to bed early and get a good night's sleep.
- Get up early enough to make a leisurely trip to the place for the test – This way unforeseen events, traffic snarls, unfamiliar buildings, etc. will not upset you.
- Dress comfortably – A written test is not a fashion show. You will be known by number and not by name, so wear something comfortable.

- Leave excess paraphernalia at home – Shopping bags and odd bundles will get in your way. You need bring only the items mentioned in the official notice you received; usually everything you need is provided. Do not bring reference books to the exam. They will only confuse those last minutes and be taken away from you when in the test room.
- Arrive somewhat ahead of time – If because of transportation schedules you must get there very early, bring a newspaper or magazine to take your mind off yourself while waiting.
- Locate the examination room – When you have found the proper room, you will be directed to the seat or part of the room where you will sit. Sometimes you are given a sheet of instructions to read while you are waiting. Do not fill out any forms until you are told to do so; just read them and be prepared.
- Relax and prepare to listen to the instructions
- If you have any physical problem that may keep you from doing your best, be sure to tell the test administrator. If you are sick or in poor health, you really cannot do your best on the exam. You can come back and take the test some other time.

## VII. AT THE TEST

The day of the test is here and you have the test booklet in your hand. The temptation to get going is very strong. Caution! There is more to success than knowing the right answers. You must know how to identify your papers and understand variations in the type of short-answer question used in this particular examination. Follow these suggestions for maximum results from your efforts:

### 1) Cooperate with the monitor
The test administrator has a duty to create a situation in which you can be as much at ease as possible. He will give instructions, tell you when to begin, check to see that you are marking your answer sheet correctly, and so on. He is not there to guard you, although he will see that your competitors do not take unfair advantage. He wants to help you do your best.

### 2) Listen to all instructions
Don't jump the gun! Wait until you understand all directions. In most civil service tests you get more time than you need to answer the questions. So don't be in a hurry. Read each word of instructions until you clearly understand the meaning. Study the examples, listen to all announcements and follow directions. Ask questions if you do not understand what to do.

### 3) Identify your papers
Civil service exams are usually identified by number only. You will be assigned a number; you must not put your name on your test papers. Be sure to copy your number correctly. Since more than one exam may be given, copy your exact examination title.

### 4) Plan your time
Unless you are told that a test is a "speed" or "rate of work" test, speed itself is usually not important. Time enough to answer all the questions will be provided, but this does not mean that you have all day. An overall time limit has been set. Divide the total time (in minutes) by the number of questions to determine the approximate time you have for each question.

## 5) Do not linger over difficult questions

If you come across a difficult question, mark it with a paper clip (useful to have along) and come back to it when you have been through the booklet. One caution if you do this – be sure to skip a number on your answer sheet as well. Check often to be sure that you have not lost your place and that you are marking in the row numbered the same as the question you are answering.

## 6) Read the questions

Be sure you know what the question asks! Many capable people are unsuccessful because they failed to *read* the questions correctly.

## 7) Answer all questions

Unless you have been instructed that a penalty will be deducted for incorrect answers, it is better to guess than to omit a question.

## 8) Speed tests

It is often better NOT to guess on speed tests. It has been found that on timed tests people are tempted to spend the last few seconds before time is called in marking answers at random – without even reading them – in the hope of picking up a few extra points. To discourage this practice, the instructions may warn you that your score will be "corrected" for guessing. That is, a penalty will be applied. The incorrect answers will be deducted from the correct ones, or some other penalty formula will be used.

## 9) Review your answers

If you finish before time is called, go back to the questions you guessed or omitted to give them further thought. Review other answers if you have time.

## 10) Return your test materials

If you are ready to leave before others have finished or time is called, take ALL your materials to the monitor and leave quietly. Never take any test material with you. The monitor can discover whose papers are not complete, and taking a test booklet may be grounds for disqualification.


## VIII. EXAMINATION TECHNIQUES

1) Read the general instructions carefully. These are usually printed on the first page of the exam booklet. As a rule, these instructions refer to the timing of the examination; the fact that you should not start work until the signal and must stop work at a signal, etc. If there are any *special* instructions, such as a choice of questions to be answered, make sure that you note this instruction carefully.

2) When you are ready to start work on the examination, that is as soon as the signal has been given, read the instructions to each question booklet, underline any key words or phrases, such as *least, best, outline, describe* and the like. In this way you will tend to answer as requested rather than discover on reviewing your paper that you *listed without describing*, that you selected the *worst* choice rather than the *best* choice, etc.

3) If the examination is of the objective or multiple-choice type – that is, each question will also give a series of possible answers: A, B, C or D, and you are called upon to select the best answer and write the letter next to that answer on your answer paper – it is advisable to start answering each question in turn. There may be anywhere from 50 to 100 such questions in the three or four hours allotted and you can see how much time would be taken if you read through all the questions before beginning to answer any. Furthermore, if you come across a question or group of questions which you know would be difficult to answer, it would undoubtedly affect your handling of all the other questions.

4) If the examination is of the essay type and contains but a few questions, it is a moot point as to whether you should read all the questions before starting to answer any one. Of course, if you are given a choice – say five out of seven and the like – then it is essential to read all the questions so you can eliminate the two that are most difficult. If, however, you are asked to answer all the questions, there may be danger in trying to answer the easiest one first because you may find that you will spend too much time on it. The best technique is to answer the first question, then proceed to the second, etc.

5) Time your answers. Before the exam begins, write down the time it started, then add the time allowed for the examination and write down the time it must be completed, then divide the time available somewhat as follows:
   - If 3-1/2 hours are allowed, that would be 210 minutes. If you have 80 objective-type questions, that would be an average of 2-1/2 minutes per question. Allow yourself no more than 2 minutes per question, or a total of 160 minutes, which will permit about 50 minutes to review.
   - If for the time allotment of 210 minutes there are 7 essay questions to answer, that would average about 30 minutes a question. Give yourself only 25 minutes per question so that you have about 35 minutes to review.

6) The most important instruction is to *read each question* and make sure you know what is wanted. The second most important instruction is to *time yourself properly* so that you answer every question. The third most important instruction is to *answer every question*. Guess if you have to but include something for each question. Remember that you will receive no credit for a blank and will probably receive some credit if you write something in answer to an essay question. If you guess a letter – say "B" for a multiple-choice question – you may have guessed right. If you leave a blank as an answer to a multiple-choice question, the examiners may respect your feelings but it will not add a point to your score. Some exams may penalize you for wrong answers, so in such cases *only*, you may not want to guess unless you have some basis for your answer.

7) Suggestions
   a. Objective-type questions
      1. Examine the question booklet for proper sequence of pages and questions
      2. Read all instructions carefully
      3. Skip any question which seems too difficult; return to it after all other questions have been answered
      4. Apportion your time properly; do not spend too much time on any single question or group of questions

5. Note and underline key words – *all, most, fewest, least, best, worst, same, opposite,* etc.
6. Pay particular attention to negatives
7. Note unusual option, e.g., unduly long, short, complex, different or similar in content to the body of the question
8. Observe the use of "hedging" words – *probably, may, most likely,* etc.
9. Make sure that your answer is put next to the same number as the question
10. Do not second-guess unless you have good reason to believe the second answer is definitely more correct
11. Cross out original answer if you decide another answer is more accurate; do not erase until you are ready to hand your paper in
12. Answer all questions; guess unless instructed otherwise
13. Leave time for review

b. Essay questions
1. Read each question carefully
2. Determine exactly what is wanted.  Underline key words or phrases.
3. Decide on outline or paragraph answer
4. Include many different points and elements unless asked to develop any one or two points or elements
5. Show impartiality by giving pros and cons unless directed to select one side only
6. Make and write down any assumptions you find necessary to answer the questions
7. Watch your English, grammar, punctuation and choice of words
8. Time your answers; don't crowd material

8) Answering the essay question

Most essay questions can be answered by framing the specific response around several key words or ideas.  Here are a few such key words or ideas:

M's: manpower, materials, methods, money, management
P's: purpose, program, policy, plan, procedure, practice, problems, pitfalls, personnel, public relations
a. Six basic steps in handling problems:
1. Preliminary plan and background development
2. Collect information, data and facts
3. Analyze and interpret information, data and facts
4. Analyze and develop solutions as well as make recommendations
5. Prepare report and sell recommendations
6. Install recommendations and follow up effectiveness

b. Pitfalls to avoid
1. *Taking things for granted –* A statement of the situation does not necessarily imply that each of the elements is necessarily true; for example, a complaint may be invalid and biased so that all that can be taken for granted is that a complaint has been registered

2. *Considering only one side of a situation* – Wherever possible, indicate several alternatives and then point out the reasons you selected the best one
3. *Failing to indicate follow up* – Whenever your answer indicates action on your part, make certain that you will take proper follow-up action to see how successful your recommendations, procedures or actions turn out to be
4. *Taking too long in answering any single question* – Remember to time your answers properly


## IX. AFTER THE TEST

Scoring procedures differ in detail among civil service jurisdictions although the general principles are the same. Whether the papers are hand-scored or graded by machine we have described, they are nearly always graded by number. That is, the person who marks the paper knows only the number – never the name – of the applicant. Not until all the papers have been graded will they be matched with names. If other tests, such as training and experience or oral interview ratings have been given, scores will be combined. Different parts of the examination usually have different weights. For example, the written test might count 60 percent of the final grade, and a rating of training and experience 40 percent. In many jurisdictions, veterans will have a certain number of points added to their grades.

After the final grade has been determined, the names are placed in grade order and an eligible list is established. There are various methods for resolving ties between those who get the same final grade – probably the most common is to place first the name of the person whose application was received first. Job offers are made from the eligible list in the order the names appear on it. You will be notified of your grade and your rank as soon as all these computations have been made. This will be done as rapidly as possible.

People who are found to meet the requirements in the announcement are called "eligibles." Their names are put on a list of eligible candidates. An eligible's chances of getting a job depend on how high he stands on this list and how fast agencies are filling jobs from the list.

When a job is to be filled from a list of eligibles, the agency asks for the names of people on the list of eligibles for that job. When the civil service commission receives this request, it sends to the agency the names of the three people highest on this list. Or, if the job to be filled has specialized requirements, the office sends the agency the names of the top three persons who meet these requirements from the general list.

The appointing officer makes a choice from among the three people whose names were sent to him. If the selected person accepts the appointment, the names of the others are put back on the list to be considered for future openings.

That is the rule in hiring from all kinds of eligible lists, whether they are for typist, carpenter, chemist, or something else. For every vacancy, the appointing officer has his choice of any one of the top three eligibles on the list. This explains why the person whose name is on top of the list sometimes does not get an appointment when some of the persons lower on the list do. If the appointing officer chooses the second or third eligible, the No. 1 eligible does not get a job at once, but stays on the list until he is appointed or the list is terminated.

## X.  HOW TO PASS THE INTERVIEW TEST

The examination for which you applied requires an oral interview test.  You have already taken the written test and you are now being called for the interview test – the final part of the formal examination.

You may think that it is not possible to prepare for an interview test and that there are no procedures to follow during an interview.  Our purpose is to point out some things you can do in advance that will help you and some good rules to follow and pitfalls to avoid while you are being interviewed.

### What is an interview supposed to test?

The written examination is designed to test the technical knowledge and competence of the candidate; the oral is designed to evaluate intangible qualities, not readily measured otherwise, and to establish a list showing the relative fitness of each candidate – as measured against his competitors – for the position sought.  Scoring is not on the basis of "right" and "wrong," but on a sliding scale of values ranging from "not passable" to "outstanding."  As a matter of fact, it is possible to achieve a relatively low score without a single "incorrect" answer because of evident weakness in the qualities being measured.

Occasionally, an examination may consist entirely of an oral test – either an individual or a group oral.  In such cases, information is sought concerning the technical knowledges and abilities of the candidate, since there has been no written examination for this purpose.  More commonly, however, an oral test is used to supplement a written examination.

### Who conducts interviews?

The composition of oral boards varies among different jurisdictions.  In nearly all, a representative of the personnel department serves as chairman.  One of the members of the board may be a representative of the department in which the candidate would work.  In some cases, "outside experts" are used, and, frequently, a businessman or some other representative of the general public is asked to serve.  Labor and management or other special groups may be represented.  The aim is to secure the services of experts in the appropriate field.

However the board is composed, it is a good idea (and not at all improper or unethical) to ascertain in advance of the interview who the members are and what groups they represent.  When you are introduced to them, you will have some idea of their backgrounds and interests, and at least you will not stutter and stammer over their names.

### What should be done before the interview?

While knowledge about the board members is useful and takes some of the surprise element out of the interview, there is other preparation which is more substantive.  It *is* possible to prepare for an oral interview – in several ways:

### 1)  Keep a copy of your application and review it carefully before the interview

This may be the only document before the oral board, and the starting point of the interview.  Know what education and experience you have listed there, and the sequence and dates of all of it.  Sometimes the board will ask you to review the highlights of your experience for them; you should not have to hem and haw doing it.

### 2)  Study the class specification and the examination announcement

Usually, the oral board has one or both of these to guide them.  The qualities, characteristics or knowledges required by the position sought are stated in these documents.  They offer valuable clues as to the nature of the oral interview.  For example, if the job involves supervisory responsibilities, the announcement will usually indicate that knowledge of modern supervisory methods and the qualifications of the candidate as a supervisor will be tested. If so, you can expect such questions, frequently in the form of a hypothetical situation which you are expected to solve. NEVER go into an oral without knowledge of the duties and responsibilities of the job you seek.

### 3) Think through each qualification required

Try to visualize the kind of questions you would ask if you were a board member. How well could you answer them? Try especially to appraise your own knowledge and background in each area, *measured against the job sought*, and identify any areas in which you are weak. Be critical and realistic – do not flatter yourself.

### 4) Do some general reading in areas in which you feel you may be weak

For example, if the job involves supervision and your past experience has NOT, some general reading in supervisory methods and practices, particularly in the field of human relations, might be useful. Do NOT study agency procedures or detailed manuals. The oral board will be testing your understanding and capacity, not your memory.

### 5) Get a good night's sleep and watch your general health and mental attitude

You will want a clear head at the interview. Take care of a cold or any other minor ailment, and of course, no hangovers.

*What should be done on the day of the interview?*

Now comes the day of the interview itself. Give yourself plenty of time to get there. Plan to arrive somewhat ahead of the scheduled time, particularly if your appointment is in the fore part of the day. If a previous candidate fails to appear, the board might be ready for you a bit early. By early afternoon an oral board is almost invariably behind schedule if there are many candidates, and you may have to wait. Take along a book or magazine to read, or your application to review, but leave any extraneous material in the waiting room when you go in for your interview. In any event, relax and compose yourself.

The matter of dress is important. The board is forming impressions about you – from your experience, your manners, your attitude, and your appearance. Give your personal appearance careful attention. Dress your best, but not your flashiest. Choose conservative, appropriate clothing, and be sure it is immaculate. This is a business interview, and your appearance should indicate that you regard it as such. Besides, being well groomed and properly dressed will help boost your confidence.

Sooner or later, someone will call your name and escort you into the interview room. *This is it.* From here on you are on your own. It is too late for any more preparation. But remember, you asked for this opportunity to prove your fitness, and you are here because your request was granted.

*What happens when you go in?*

The usual sequence of events will be as follows: The clerk (who is often the board stenographer) will introduce you to the chairman of the oral board, who will introduce you to the other members of the board. Acknowledge the introductions before you sit down. Do not be surprised if you find a microphone facing you or a stenotypist sitting by. Oral interviews are usually recorded in the event of an appeal or other review.

Usually the chairman of the board will open the interview by reviewing the highlights of your education and work experience from your application – primarily for the benefit of the other members of the board, as well as to get the material into the record. Do not interrupt or comment unless there is an error or significant misinterpretation; if that is the case, do not hesitate. But do not quibble about insignificant matters. Also, he will usually ask you some question about your education, experience or your present job – partly to get you to start talking and to establish the interviewing "rapport." He may start the actual questioning, or turn it over to one of the other members. Frequently, each member undertakes the questioning on a particular area, one in which he is perhaps most competent, so you can expect each member to participate in the examination. Because time is limited, you may also expect some rather abrupt switches in the direction the questioning takes, so do not be upset by it. Normally, a board member will not pursue a single line of questioning unless he discovers a particular strength or weakness.

After each member has participated, the chairman will usually ask whether any member has any further questions, then will ask you if you have anything you wish to add. Unless you are expecting this question, it may floor you. Worse, it may start you off on an extended, extemporaneous speech. The board is not usually seeking more information. The question is principally to offer you a last opportunity to present further qualifications or to indicate that you have nothing to add. So, if you feel that a significant qualification or characteristic has been overlooked, it is proper to point it out in a sentence or so. Do not compliment the board on the thoroughness of their examination – they have been sketchy, and you know it. If you wish, merely say, "No thank you, I have nothing further to add." This is a point where you can "talk yourself out" of a good impression or fail to present an important bit of information. Remember, *you close the interview yourself.*

The chairman will then say, "That is all, Mr. _____, thank you." Do not be startled; the interview is over, and quicker than you think. Thank him, gather your belongings and take your leave. Save your sigh of relief for the other side of the door.

*How to put your best foot forward*

Throughout this entire process, you may feel that the board individually and collectively is trying to pierce your defenses, seek out your hidden weaknesses and embarrass and confuse you. Actually, this is not true. They are obliged to make an appraisal of your qualifications for the job you are seeking, and they want to see you in your best light. Remember, they must interview all candidates and a non-cooperative candidate may become a failure in spite of their best efforts to bring out his qualifications. Here are 15 suggestions that will help you:

**1) Be natural – Keep your attitude confident, not cocky**

If you are not confident that you can do the job, do not expect the board to be. Do not apologize for your weaknesses, try to bring out your strong points. The board is interested in a positive, not negative, presentation. Cockiness will antagonize any board member and make him wonder if you are covering up a weakness by a false show of strength.

**2) Get comfortable, but don't lounge or sprawl**

Sit erectly but not stiffly. A careless posture may lead the board to conclude that you are careless in other things, or at least that you are not impressed by the importance of the occasion. Either conclusion is natural, even if incorrect. Do not fuss with your clothing, a pencil or an ashtray. Your hands may occasionally be useful to emphasize a point; do not let them become a point of distraction.

**3) Do not wisecrack or make small talk**

This is a serious situation, and your attitude should show that you consider it as such. Further, the time of the board is limited – they do not want to waste it, and neither should you.

## 4) Do not exaggerate your experience or abilities

In the first place, from information in the application or other interviews and sources, the board may know more about you than you think. Secondly, you probably will not get away with it. An experienced board is rather adept at spotting such a situation, so do not take the chance.

## 5) If you know a board member, do not make a point of it, yet do not hide it

Certainly you are not fooling him, and probably not the other members of the board. Do not try to take advantage of your acquaintanceship – it will probably do you little good.

## 6) Do not dominate the interview

Let the board do that. They will give you the clues – do not assume that you have to do all the talking. Realize that the board has a number of questions to ask you, and do not try to take up all the interview time by showing off your extensive knowledge of the answer to the first one.

## 7) Be attentive

You only have 20 minutes or so, and you should keep your attention at its sharpest throughout. When a member is addressing a problem or question to you, give him your undivided attention. Address your reply principally to him, but do not exclude the other board members.

## 8) Do not interrupt

A board member may be stating a problem for you to analyze. He will ask you a question when the time comes. Let him state the problem, and wait for the question.

## 9) Make sure you understand the question

Do not try to answer until you are sure what the question is. If it is not clear, restate it in your own words or ask the board member to clarify it for you. However, do not haggle about minor elements.

## 10) Reply promptly but not hastily

A common entry on oral board rating sheets is "candidate responded readily," or "candidate hesitated in replies." Respond as promptly and quickly as you can, but do not jump to a hasty, ill-considered answer.

## 11) Do not be peremptory in your answers

A brief answer is proper – but do not fire your answer back. That is a losing game from your point of view. The board member can probably ask questions much faster than you can answer them.

## 12) Do not try to create the answer you think the board member wants

He is interested in what kind of mind you have and how it works – not in playing games. Furthermore, he can usually spot this practice and will actually grade you down on it.

## 13) Do not switch sides in your reply merely to agree with a board member

Frequently, a member will take a contrary position merely to draw you out and to see if you are willing and able to defend your point of view. Do not start a debate, yet do not surrender a good position. If a position is worth taking, it is worth defending.

## 14) Do not be afraid to admit an error in judgment if you are shown to be wrong

The board knows that you are forced to reply without any opportunity for careful consideration. Your answer may be demonstrably wrong. If so, admit it and get on with the interview.

## 15) Do not dwell at length on your present job

The opening question may relate to your present assignment. Answer the question but do not go into an extended discussion. You are being examined for a *new* job, not your present one. As a matter of fact, try to phrase ALL your answers in terms of the job for which you are being examined.

*Basis of Rating*

Probably you will forget most of these "do's" and "don'ts" when you walk into the oral interview room. Even remembering them all will not ensure you a passing grade. Perhaps you did not have the qualifications in the first place. But remembering them will help you to put your best foot forward, without treading on the toes of the board members.

Rumor and popular opinion to the contrary notwithstanding, an oral board wants you to make the best appearance possible. They know you are under pressure – but they also want to see how you respond to it as a guide to what your reaction would be under the pressures of the job you seek. They will be influenced by the degree of poise you display, the personal traits you show and the manner in which you respond.

ABOUT THIS BOOK

This book contains tests divided into Examination Sections. Go through each test, answering every question in the margin. We have also attached a sample answer sheet at the back of the book that can be removed and used. At the end of each test look at the answer key and check your answers. On the ones you got wrong, look at the right answer choice and learn. Do not fill in the answers first. Do not memorize the questions and answers, but understand the answer and principles involved. On your test, the questions will likely be different from the samples. Questions are changed and new ones added. If you understand these past questions you should have success with any changes that arise. Tests may consist of several types of questions. We have additional books on each subject should more study be advisable or necessary for you. Finally, the more you study, the better prepared you will be. This book is intended to be the last thing you study before you walk into the examination room. Prior study of relevant texts is also recommended. NLC publishes some of these in our Fundamental Series. Knowledge and good sense are important factors in passing your exam. Good luck also helps. So now study this Passbook, absorb the material contained within and take that knowledge into the examination. Then do your best to pass that exam.

---

# EXAMINATION SECTION

# EXAMINATION SECTION
## TEST 1

DIRECTIONS: Each question or incomplete statement is followed by several suggested answers or completions. Select the one that BEST answers the question or completes the statement. *PRINT THE LETTER OF THE CORRECT ANSWER IN THE SPACE AT THE RIGHT.*

1. The one of the following entrees which offers the LEAST variation in texture is          1.____

   A. turkey, cranberry sauce, fried golden brown potatoes, peas
   B. chopped sirloin, mushroom gravy, French fried potatoes broccoli spears
   C. oven-fried chicken, baked potato, peas and carrots, salad
   D. meat loaf, mashed potatoes, creamed spinach, white bread

2. In planning a menu, the FIRST item which should be chosen is the          2.____

   A. vegetable          B. salad          C. entree          D. dessert

3. Of the following, the BEST method of tenderizing cuts of meat which are less tender is by          3.____

   A. broiling          B. stewing          C. baking          D. deep-frying

4. Which one of the following statements regarding proteins is CORRECT?          4.____

   A. The amount of protein in the body is a constant.
   B. The presence of nitrogen distinguishes protein from carbohydrates and fat.
   C. Protein provides more calories per gram than carbohydrates or fat.
   D. Protein provides the principal source of glucose to brain tissue.

5. The one of the following foods that provides MORE vitamin C per serving than the others is          5.____

   A. brussels sprouts                    B. cabbage
   C. tomatoes                            D. turnips

6. Liver is a PRIMARY source of which one of the following vitamins?          6.____

   A. A          B. $B_6$          C. C          D. D

7. Vitamin A is a fat soluble vitamin essential in an adequate diet for children and adults. Which one of the following statements concerning vitamin A is TRUE?          7.____

   A. The Recommended Daily Allowance for vitamin A for the adult male and female 10 years of age and older is the same.
   B. The Recommended Daily Allowance for vitamin A is expressed in terms of U.S.P. units.
   C. Vegetables have vitamin A activity equal to vitamin A in animal foods.
   D. Excessive amounts of vitamin A are well tolerated by adults.

8. Iron is a mineral required for growth and to keep the body functioning properly. Of the following, the combination of foods that will provide the BEST intake of iron is          8.____

   A. green peas, liver, enriched bread, dried potatoes
   B. cheese, oranges, liver, butter

C. peanut butter, milk, carrots, liver
D. liver, ice cream, chicken, peaches

9. Calcium and phosphorous account for approximately three-fourths of the mineral elements in the body. Their intake is important for adequate nutrition.
Which one of the following statements is CORRECT about both minerals?

A. For children and young adults, the Recommended Daily Allowance for calcium is twice that for phosphorous.
B. Their absorption and utilization are enhanced by the presence of vitamin E.
C. They are not found in soft tissues.
D. They constitute an important buffer system in the regulation of body neutrality.

9.___

10. When a menu is being planned for a specific holiday, the one of the following which is LEAST appropriate is to

A. ask for suitable menu possibilities from the staff
B. choose only foods which are familiar to those who will be served
C. test acceptability of possible holiday items by serving one or two items at earlier meals
D. include traditional foods associated with the holiday, if available

10.___

11. When a No. 8 scoop is used to serve mashed potatoes, the portion served should be _____ cup.

A. 2/5        B. 1/3        C. 1/2        D. 2/3

11.___

12. A six-ounce ladle is equal to APPROXIMATELY _____ cup(s).

A. 1/2        B. 1        C. 3/4        D. 1 1/4

12.___

13. The MOST accurate measurement of food is by

A. volume
B. weight
C. can size
D. number of pieces per container

13.___

14. Deep fat frying is BEST accomplished at which one of the following temperatures?

A. 300° F        B. 350° F        C. 400° F        D. 450° F

14.___

15. When you are roasting beef, the indication that a well-done and palatable product has been achieved is an interior temperature in the range of

A. 110° to 130° F        B. 131° to 150° F
C. 151° to 170° F        D. 171° to 190° F

15.___

16. Of the following methods of roasting beef, the one that causes the LEAST amount of shrinkage is cooking at

A. high temperature during the first half of the cooking time and at low temperature during the other half
B. high temperature during the entire cooking time

16.___

C. moderate temperature during the first half of the cooking time and at high temperature during the other half

D. low temperature during the entire cooking time

17. The method of meat preparation that calls for cutting the meat into small pieces, covering with hot liquid, and cooking at about 185° F is known as    17.____

    A. boiling         B. stewing        C. roasting        D. broiling

18. Of the following pressure ranges, the one in which three compartment steamers operate is the _____ lb. range.    18.____

    A. 1-5           B. 5-15          C. 15-30        D. 30-50

19. When vegetables are cooked for large numbers of people, the BEST results are obtained by *batch cooking.*    19.____
This kind of cooking is done in order to

    A. have high-quality vegetables available during the entire serving period
    B. prepare more vegetables using less staff
    C. use less equipment
    D. prepare several batches of vegetables at the same time

20. The one of the following procedures that could cause food poisoning is    20.____

    A. allowing cooked poultry to stand for an hour, slicing it, and covering it with broth, and holding it at room temperature for several hours
    B. keeping food mixtures on cafeteria counters for one hour
    C. cooking left-over food mixtures quickly by frequent stirring and then refrigerating in shallow pans
    D. chilling all ingredients for salads for at least one hour before preparation

21. When large numbers of people are to be served in a cafeteria setting, an estimate should be made each day of the quantity of food to be prepared and cooked.    21.____
This is BEST done by which one of the following ways?

    A. Having the cook make a list of the previous day's leftovers.
    B. Considering previous sales of the same menu combinations, as well as the weather and any special events.
    C. Cooking as much food as the staff and equipment allow so as not to be caught short.
    D. Using the capacity of the seating area as a base.

22. Which one of the following statements concerning frozen pre-cooked foods is NOT correct?    22.____

    A. Certain pre-cooked foods are excellent when freshly prepared, but deteriorate rapidly in an ordinary freezer.
    B. Some pre-cooked foods are so greatly changed by freezing and subsequent reheating that they become unpalatable.
    C. All food items which are carefully cooked, rapidly frozen, and then held at low temperature until used, are satisfactory products when served.
    D. Many foods may be frozen, stored in an appropriate type of freezer, and thawed without marked change in nutritional and esthetic value.

23. Of the following, the one which is NOT a method of controlling food costs in an institu-    23.____
tional food service is

  A.  avoiding the use of *leftover* foods since they are usually unpopular items
  B.  maintaining an accurate food inventory
  C.  knowing what yield can be obtained from various sizes, counts, and amounts of
      food
  D.  ensuring the food-service employees use standardized recipes and portions

24. The direct labor cost involved in the preparation of meals includes wages paid to cooks,    24.____
bakers, salad makers, counter workers, etc. and is MOST accurately determined by
which one of the following methods?

  A.  Making studies of the amount of time spent by employees in actual meal prepara-
      tion tasks.
  B.  Checking employees' time cards to determine total absence time.
  C.  Dividing the number of meals served each week by the number of employees.
  D.  Determining how much time is lost because of equipment breakdown and adding
      the value of this time to the cost of employees' wages.

25. Which one of the following would MOST likely enable the supervisor of a food service to    25.____
attain better cost control over operations?

  A.  *Increasing* the output of individual staff members.
  B.  *Increasing* the size of the staff.
  C.  *Reducing* the amount of time scheduled for food preparation tasks.
  D.  *Reducing* the amount of time spent on training staff members.

―――――

# KEY (CORRECT ANSWERS)

| | | | | |
|---|---|---|---|---|
| 1. | D | | 11. | C |
| 2. | C | | 12. | C |
| 3. | B | | 13. | B |
| 4. | B | | 14. | B |
| 5. | A | | 15. | D |
| | | | | |
| 6. | A | | 16. | D |
| 7. | A | | 17. | B |
| 8. | A | | 18. | B |
| 9. | D | | 19. | A |
| 10. | B | | 20. | A |

| | |
|---|---|
| 21. | B |
| 22. | C |
| 23. | A |
| 24. | A |
| 25. | A |

―――――

# TEST 2

DIRECTIONS: Each question or incomplete statement is followed by several suggested answers or completions. Select the one that BEST answers the question or completes the statement. *PRINT THE LETTER OF THE CORRECT ANSWER IN THE SPACE AT THE RIGHT.*

1. Of the following, the FIRST step in the control of food costs in an institution should be to          1.\_\_\_\_

   A. make sure the delivery of foods is in accordance with the order
   B. store foods under tight security as soon as they are received
   C. follow purchase specifications in obtaining food products
   D. get the correct amount of raw food to the cook

2. Of the following, the area in which recipe costing aids are of MOST value is          2.\_\_\_\_

   A. making yield studies
   B. planning menus
   C. taking inventories
   D. determining the cost of wasted foods

3. Control records of both the physical and cost aspects of food storage are MOST useful as a basic guide in which one of the following areas?          3.\_\_\_\_

   A. Receiving food deliveries          B. Issuing food to the kitchen
   C. Ordering food          D. Controlling food theft

4. The one of the following which indicates actual control over food costs in a food service is that          4.\_\_\_\_

   A. recipe costing is done
   B. waste is eliminated
   C. yield studies are made
   D. food cost data are regularly analyzed

5. The one of the following which is the MAJOR purpose of a perpetual inventory in the food storage area of a kitchen or other dietary unit is to          5.\_\_\_\_

   A. facilitate removal of shelf items that are needed for quick use
   B. reduce breakage and spoilage of liquified foods
   C. act as a control in the area of food purchasing
   D. facilitate the planning of balanced diets and menus

6. Walk-in storage refrigerators can be a very important aspect of a well-equipped kitchen in a food service.
   Of the following, the MOST desirable location for a walk-in refrigerator is near the          6.\_\_\_\_

   A. receiving and preparation areas
   B. tray delivery area
   C. cafeteria
   D. dishwashing area

7. Food specifications are precise statements of quality and other commodity requirements. 7.___
All food should be purchased according to specifications.
Of the following, the LEAST important aspect of a food specification is the

   A. quantity required in a case, pound, carton, etc.
   B. federal grade desired
   C. size of the container
   D. picture of the item

8. The aim in buying food is to obtain the best value for the money spent. 8.___
Of the following, the practice which is LEAST likely to accomplish that aim is

   A. buying the cheapest item
   B. purchasing by specification
   C. purchasing only the quantities required for the menus planned
   D. checking all purchases on delivery

9. When deciding whether to select a particular piece of equipment for a kitchen or other 9.___
dietary area, the one of the following which would be LEAST important for you to take
into consideration is

   A. whether there is space for it
   B. whether it is easily cleaned and maintained
   C. whether there is an employee currently on staff who knows how to operate it
   D. how well it has worked in other institutions

10. Of the following foods, the type that is MOST likely to cause staph food poisoning if 10.___
improperly prepared or handled is _____ food.

   A. sugar-coated                    B. dried
   C. pickled                         D. cream-filled

11. Harmful bacteria are MOST often introduced into foods prepared in a food service oper- 11.___
ation by

   A. insects          B. rodents          C. employees          D. utensils

12. When planning menus for secondary school students, it is desirable for the manager to 12.___
do all of the following EXCEPT to

   A. stay within the school's food budget
   B. include familiar ethnic foods
   C. include many food choices
   D. consider the size of the food service staff

13. Of the following, the manager's BEST evidence for a shortage claim on surplus food 13.___
delivered to a school is

   A. her written report of the shortage claim
   B. the delivery receipt from the truck driver
   C. the container the food was delivered in
   D. an old container of the same item

14. The manager should prepare school lunch menus for a MINIMUM of _____ week(s) at a time.   14._____

    A.  one          B.  two          C.  three          D.  four

15. The manager must keep monthly inventories of all of the following EXCEPT   15._____

    A.  paper goods                 B.  food items
    C.  serving utensils            D.  cleaning supplies

16. In the Type A lunch pattern for 10- to 12-year-old children, all of the following fulfill the *meat or meat alternate* requirement EXCEPT   16._____

    A.  two ounces of cheese
    B.  one-half cup of fresh carrots
    C.  four tablespoons of peanut butter
    D.  one-half cup of cooked dry peas

17. A manager is planning to use tuna fish salad to comply with the guideline for the *meat or meat alternate* requirement of the Type A lunch for secondary school students. How much tuna fish will she need in order to serve 400 secondary school students? _____ pounds.   17._____

    A.  $37\frac{1}{2}$          B.  50          C.  75          D.  100

Questions 18-25.

DIRECTIONS:    Answer Questions 18 through 25 SOLELY on the basis of information presented in the charts below.

### STUDENT SALES COUNTER SHEET
#### March 4, 2005

| Item | Price per Item | No. Items Offered for Sale | No. Items Unsold | Total Cash Received for Items Sold |
|---|---|---|---|---|
| Hot lunch | $2.25 | 250 | 75 | |
| Milk | $0.60 | 525 | | $285.00 |
| Soda | $0.75 | 300 | 163 | $102.75 |
| Ice Cream Bars | $0.45 | 181 | 59 | $54.90 |
| Buttered Roll | $0.15 | 200 | 150 | |
| Cooked Vegetable | $0.90 | 325 | 40 | $256.50 |
| Pudding | $0.45 | 565 | 30 | $240.75 |
| Potato Chips | $0.30 | 610 | 50 | $168.00 |

## STUDENT SALES COUNTER SHEET
### March 5, 2005

| Item | Price per Item | No. Items Offered for Sale | No. Items Unsold | Total Cash Received for Items Sold |
|---|---|---|---|---|
| Hot lunch | $2.25 | 300 | | $585.00 |
| Milk | $0.60 | 450 | | $255.00 |
| Soda | $0.75 | 275 | 207 | |
| Ice Cream Bars | $0.45 | 250 | 100 | |
| Buttered Roll | $0.15 | 175 | 25 | |
| Cooked Vegetable | $0.90 | 300 | 62 | $214.20 |
| Pudding | $0.45 | 490 | 47 | |
| Potato Chips | $0.30 | 595 | 45 | |

18. Hot lunches accounted for APPROXIMATELY what percentage of all cash received for March 4, 2005?

    A.  10%        B.  15%        C.  20%        D.  25%

18.___

19. Which one of the following items was sold LEAST on March 4, 2005 and March 5, 2005, combined?

    A.  Soda                    B.  Ice cream bars
    C.  Buttered roll           D.  Cooked vegetable

19.___

20. The number of milk containers which were unsold on March 4, 2005 is

    A.  30        B.  50        C.  75        D.  95

20.___

21. How many fewer containers of pudding and soda were sold on March 5, 2005 than were sold on March 4, 2005?

    A.  19        B.  81        C.  105        D.  161

21.___

22. Which single item, besides hot lunches, accounted for the GREATEST number of items sold on March 4, 2005?

    A.  Cooked vegetable        B.  Pudding
    C.  Ice cream bars          D.  Soda

22.___

23. How many hot lunches were sold on March 4, 2005 and March 5, 2005, combined?

    A.  435        B.  550        C.  625        D.  665

23.___

24. Of the following, the item that was bought MOST by the students on both March 4, 2005 and March 5, 2005 is

    A.  soda                    B.  buttered roll
    C.  pudding                 D.  potato chips

24.___

25. The cumulative total of money received for all the soda, ice cream bars, buttered rolls, and pudding sold on March 4, 2005 is

    A.  $165.15        B.  $405.90        C.  $858.90        D.  $1252.65

25.___

# KEY (CORRECT ANSWERS)

| | | | | |
|---|---|---|---|---|
| 1. | C | | 11. | C |
| 2. | B | | 12. | C |
| 3. | C | | 13. | C |
| 4. | B | | 14. | D |
| 5. | C | | 15. | C |
| | | | | |
| 6. | A | | 16. | B |
| 7. | D | | 17. | C |
| 8. | A | | 18. | D |
| 9. | C | | 19. | C |
| 10. | D | | 20. | B |

21. D
22. B
23. A
24. D
25. B

———

# EXAMINATION SECTION
## TEST 1

DIRECTIONS:    Each question or incomplete statement is followed by several suggested answers or completions. Select the one that BEST answers the question or completes the statement. *PRINT THE LETTER OF THE CORRECT ANSWER IN THE SPACE AT THE RIGHT.*

1. In food service operations, the supervisor usually can arrive at a decision concerning an operations problem by considering the following steps to a solution:
   I.   Analysis of available information
   II.  Definition of problem
   III. Development of alternate solutions
   IV.  Selection of decision
   In which of the following options are the steps given in PROPER sequence?

    A.  II, I, III, IV               B.  I, III, II, IV
    C.  I, II, III, IV               D.  III, I, II, IV

1.____

2. The one of the following which is MOST important for improvement of the productivity of food-service employees is the

    A.  use of convenience foods
    B.  posting of food preparation schedules for employees
    C.  adoption and implementation of a program of task analysis and work measurement
    D.  advance preparation of as much food as possible

2.____

3. Assume that all of the following problems are occurring in a kitchen under your supervision: production is slow in terms of food preparation; housekeeping is lax; the quality of the food prepared is very poor; morale is low.
   Of these four problems, the one that is *most likely* the cause of all the others and should probably be attended to FIRST is

    A.  slow production             B.  lax housekeeping
    C.  poorly prepared food       D.  low morale

3.____

4. A common problem in food-service supervision is that improper supervisory practices can lead to situations in which subordinates disobey direct orders given to them by their superior.
   Which of the following supervisors would be *most likely* to promote such a situation? A supervisor who

    A.  does not delegate authority
    B.  does not make a decision without consulting his or her entire staff
    C.  is unwilling to punish any employee for an infraction of the rules
    D.  rarely holds meetings with his or her staff

4.____

5. While reviewing kitchen operations, you notice that a recently-hired employee is using too large a scoop for serving mashed potatoes. Since you personally instructed this individual in the proper utilization of serving utensils, you believe that this employee should be reprimanded.
   In this situation, the *most appropriate* of the following actions would be to

5.____

A. call the employee aside, inform him of his mistake, and plan for additional instruction
B. inform the employee of his mistake in the presence of the other employees
C. remove the employee from his work station and assign him to some less desirable tasks
D. assign another employee to serve the mashed potatoes with the appropriate size scoop and have the recently-hired employee observe

6. Assume that you are approached individually by two employees who work together in food preparation. Each employee registers her complaint against working with the other. Which one of the following would be the MOST effective action to take in order to handle this problem?    6.___

A. At the next regularly scheduled staff meeting, mention the importance of good working relationships.
B. Ask your superior to make a judgment in this case, instead of deciding what to do yourself.
C. Reassign one employee to a suitable job where she will not have to work with the other employee.
D. Write a report to your superior detailing the problem and requesting transfers for both of the employees.

7. Suppose that, as a supervisor, you have an idea for changing the way a certain task is performed by your staff so that it will be less tedious and get done faster.
Of the following, the MOST advisable action for you to take regarding this idea is to    7.___

A. issue a written memorandum, explaining the new method and giving reasons why it is to replace the old one
B. discuss it with your staff to get their reactions and suggestions
C. set up a training class in the new method for your staff
D. try it out on an experimental basis on half the staff

8. In preparing work schedules for food-service employees, the one of the following considerations to which the supervisor should give LEAST priority is the    8.___

A. work skills of the employees
B. jobs to be done
C. physical set-up of the work area and equipment available
D. preferences of the employees

9. A new employee complains to you that she thinks the current method of serving meals is very ineffective. This employee strongly insists that another method is much better. However, the suggested method had been tried in the past with very unsatisfactory results. Of the following, the BEST way for you to handle the situation would be to    9.___

A. assign the employee to a different work area to avoid conflict
B. try out the suggested method for one or two days to demonstrate why it doesn't work
C. briefly tell the employee that her suggested method will not work
D. discuss with the employee the reasons why the present method has proven to be more successful than her suggested method

10. Assume that you find it necessary to discipline two subordinates, Mr. Tate and Mr. Sawyer, for coming to work late on several occasions. Their latenesses have had disruptive effects on the work schedule, and you have given both of them several verbal warnings. Mr. Tate has been in your work unit for many years, and his work has always been satisfactory. Mr. Sawyer is a probationary employee who has had some problems in learning your procedures. You decide to give Mr. Tate one more warning, in private, for his latenesses.
According to good supervisory practice, which one of the following disciplinary actions should you take with regard to Mr. Sawyer?

   A. Give him a reprimand in front of his co-workers to make a lasting impression.
   B. Recommend dismissal since he has not yet completed his probationary period.
   C. Give him one more warning, in private, for his latenesses.
   D. Recommend a short suspension or payroll deduction to impress on him the importance of coming to work on time.

11. Assume that you have delegated a very important work assignment to Johnson, one of your most experienced subordinates. Prior to completion of the assignment, your superior accidentally discovers that the assignment is being carried out incorrectly and tells you about it.
Which one of the following responses is *most appropriate* for you to give to your superior?

   A. "I take full responsibility, and I will see to it that the assignment is carried out correctly."
   B. "Johnson has been with us for many years now and should know better."
   C. "It really isn't Johnson's fault, rather it is the fault of the ancient equipment we have to do the job."
   D. "I think you should inform Johnson since he is the one at fault, not I."

12. Assume that you observe that one of your employees is talking excessively with other employees, quitting early and taking unusually long rest periods. Despite these abuses, she is one of your most productive employees, and her work is usually of the highest quality.
Of the following, the *most appropriate* action to take with regard to this employee is to

   A. ignore these infractions since she is one of your best workers
   B. ask your superior to reprimand her so that you can remain on the employee's good side
   C. reprimand her since not doing so would lower the morale of the other employees
   D. ask another of your subordinates to mention these infractions to the offending employee and suggest that she stop breaking rules

13. Assume that you have noticed that an employee whose attendance had been quite satisfactory is now showing marked evidence of a consistent pattern of absences.
Of the following, the BEST way to cope with this problem is to

   A. wait several weeks to see whether this pattern continues
   B. meet with the employee to try to find out the reasons for this change
   C. call a staff meeting and discuss the need for good attendance
   D. write a carefully worded warning to the employee

14. It is generally agreed that the successful supervisor must know how to wisely delegate work to her subordinates since she cannot do everything herself.
Which one of the following practices is *most likely* to result in INEFFECTIVE delegation by a supervisor?

    A. Establishment of broad controls to assure feedback about any deviations from plans
    B. Willingness to let subordinates use their own ideas about how to get the job done, where appropriate
    C. Constant observance of employees to see if they are making any mistakes
    D. Granting of enough authority to make possible the accomplishment of the delegated work

14.___

15. Suppose that, in accordance with grievance procedures, an employee brings a complaint to you, his immediate supervisor.
In dealing with his complaint, the one of the following which is MOST important for you to do is to

    A. talk to the employee's co-workers to learn whether the complaint is justified
    B. calm the employee by assuring him that you will look into the matter as soon as possible
    C. tell your immediate superior about the employee's complaint
    D. give the employee an opportunity to tell the full story

15.___

16. The successful application by a supervisor of work simplification techniques to food preparation and service work is *most likely* to result in which one of the following?

    A. Employees working harder than before
    B. Food products of higher nutritional value
    C. Better employee attendance
    D. Elimination of unnecessary parts of jobs

16.___

17. Holding staff meetings at regular Intervals is generally considered to be a good supervisory practice.
Which one of the following subjects is LEAST desirable for discussion at such a meeting?

    A. Revisions in agency personnel policies
    B. Violation of an agency rule by one of the employees present
    C. Problems of waste and breakage in the work area
    D. Complaints of employees about working conditions

17.___

18. Suppose that you are informed that your staff is soon to be reduced by one-third due to budget problems.
Which one of the following steps would be LEAST advisable in your effort to maintain a quality service with the smaller number of employees?

    A. Directing employees to speed up operations
    B. Giving employees training or retraining
    C. Rearranging the work area
    D. Revising work methods

18.___

19. Of the following, which action on the part of the supervisor is LEAST likely to contribute to upgrading the skills of her subordinates?    19.____

    A. Providing appropriate training to subordinates
    B. Making periodic evaluations of subordinates and discussing the evaluations with the subordinates
    C. Consistently assigning subordinates to those tasks with which they are familiar
    D. Giving increased responsibility to appropriate subordinates

20. Suppose that a new employee on your staff has difficulty in performing his assigned tasks, after having been given training.    20.____
Of the following courses of action, the one which would be BEST for you, his supervisor, to take FIRST is to

    A. change his work assignment
    B. give him a poor evaluation since he is obviously unable to do the work
    C. give him the training again
    D. have him work with an employee who is more experienced in the tasks for a short while

21. To insure the safety of employees who must retrieve items from a food storeroom, the supervisor should direct that    21.____

    A. bulky items be put on the floor near the storeroom door
    B. newly-received items be put on the shelves in front of previously-received items
    C. ladders or step-stools be used to reach upper shelves
    D. frequently-requisitioned items be piled up just outside the entrance to the storeroom

22. Suppose that a cook receives a minor burn, which causes a blister on his hand, while handling a hot pan of food. After seeing that the employee gets proper treatment for the burn, the MOST advisable of the following actions for the supervisor to take is to    22.____

    A. send the employee home
    B. tell the employee to return to his work station
    C. help the employee to finish the day's food preparation
    D. temporarily assign the employee to a task other than handling food

23. Of the following, the FIRST step which should be taken by you, the supervisor, in the orientation of a new food-service employee is to    23.____

    A. include the new employee in the next regularly-scheduled staff conference
    B. discuss with the new employee the many problems which the kitchen staff faces daily
    C. give the new employee a task to see how well he can perform
    D. have a conference with the new employee and discuss what his duties will be

24. Assume that, as part of a step-by-step training process, the supervisor explained and demonstrated a food preparation task to a new employee. As a last step, the supervisor told the employee to perform the task himself.    24.____
The training given by this supervisor was

A. *good;* by putting the employee on his own, the supervisor indicated confidence in the employee
B. *poor;* he didn't ask whether the employee understood how to perform the task
C. *good;* he employed the technique of demonstration
D. *poor;* more than one instructor is required to make this method of training effective

25. Of the following, the BEST way to follow-up immediately after giving a new employee training in food preparation tasks is to

    A. have the new employee observe more experienced employees performing their tasks
    B. give the new employee an overall view of all the food service operations
    C. allow the new employee to perform the tasks herself under careful supervision
    D. have the new employee write a report on what she has learned

25.___

26. If one of your kitchen staff performs a particularly important task incorrectly, the one of the following times which is BEST for teaching her the proper procedure so that she will remember it is

    A. later on in the day after she has had time to think about the task
    B. immediately so that she can correct her error
    C. after the workday ends so you may speak to her with less distraction
    D. during the next regularly-scheduled staff training session

26.___

27. Assume that you are approached by a cook who is upset and who wants to give you her explanation as to why the day's food preparation went wrong.
In order to be an understanding listener, you should do ALL of the following EXCEPT

    A. carefully question the worker
    B. make a value judgment so you can take a definite position on the matter
    C. try to find out the meaning of the emotions behind the cook's statements
    D. restate the cook's position to assure that you comprehend what she is telling you

27.___

28. A troubled subordinate privately approaches his supervisor in order to talk about a problem on the job.
In this situation, the one of the following actions that is NOT desirable on the part of the supervisor is to

    A. ask the subordinate pertinent questions to help develop points further
    B. close his office door during the talk to block noisy distractions
    C. allow sufficient time to complete the discussion with the subordinate
    D. take over the conversation so the employee won't be embarrassed

28.___

29. Suppose that one of your goals as a supervisor is to foster good working relationships between yourself and your employees, without undermining your supervisory effectiveness by being too friendly.
Of the following, the BEST way to achieve this goal when dealing with employees' work problems is to

    A. discourage individual personal conferences by using regularly scheduled staff meetings to discuss work problems
    B. try to resolve work problems within a relatively short period of time

29.___

C. insist that employees put all work problems into writing before seeing you
D. maintain an open-door policy, allowing employees complete freedom of access to you without making appointments to discuss work problems

30. Of the following duties, the one that may be performed by a designated employee instead of the manager is      30.____

    A. preparing work schedules for each job in the kitchen
    B. placing all orders for food
    C. checking, counting, and weighing supplies received
    D. tasting all cooked foods, salads, sandwich and dessert mixtures

———

# KEY (CORRECT ANSWERS)

| | | | | | |
|---|---|---|---|---|---|
| 1. | A | 11. | A | 21. | C |
| 2. | C | 12. | C | 22. | D |
| 3. | D | 13. | B | 23. | D |
| 4. | C | 14. | C | 24. | B |
| 5. | A | 15. | D | 25. | C |
| 6. | C | 16. | D | 26. | B |
| 7. | B | 17. | B | 27. | B |
| 8. | D | 18. | A | 28. | D |
| 9. | D | 19. | C | 29. | B |
| 10. | C | 20. | D | 30. | C |

———

# EXAMINATION SECTION
## TEST 1

DIRECTIONS: Each question or incomplete statement is followed by several suggested answers or completions. Select the one that BEST answers the question or completes the statement. *PRINT THE LETTER OF THE CORRECT ANSWER IN THE SPACE AT THE RIGHT.*

1. Of the following, the requisition which is CORRECT for the number of servings indicated is

    A. 300 lbs. eviscerated frozen turkey for 480 servings
    B. 190 lbs. cured ham, bone in, for ham steaks for 600 servilngs
    C. 100 lbs. whole beef liver for 520 servings
    D. 380 lbs. veal leg, bone in, for roast veal for 500 servings

1.____

2. Of the following, the LEAST effective way of effecting portion control is by means of

    A. instruction of personnel responsible for serving food
    B. purchase of pre-portioned foods
    C. use of standardized serving utensils
    D. preparation and use of standardized recipes

2.____

3. The MOST important reason for using a manual in a dietary department is that it serves as a

    A. means of preventing duplication of work
    B. tool for achieving orderly operations
    C. system for controlling food waste
    D. system for controlling food costs

3.____

4. Of the following, the MOST important reason for using standardized recipes is that they provide

    A. uniformity of quality and quantity of the product
    B. greater control of raw food costs
    C. saving of labor hours resulting in lower cost
    D. guidance in pre-planning of menus

4.____

5. From the standpoint of the dietitian, the CHIEF advantage of centralized as compared to decentralized food service is that

    A. space needed for floor pantries in a decentralized service can be used instead for other purposes
    B. better controls can be exercised by the dietitian
    C. less service is required from the nursing department
    D. it eliminates complaints that pantry noises on the floor disturb the patients

5.____

6. Assume that the dishwashing load is unusually heavy for the facilities provided. Of the following, the MOST expedient method for reducing the load would be to

    A. stagger the meal hours
    B. use paper cups for beverages

6.____

C. increase the number of employees handling the operation
D. decrease the timing on the machine wash and rinse operations

7. The amount of freezer space necessary in a kitchen will depend MAINLY upon the 7.____

A. frequency of delivery service
B. amount of money that can be tied up in stored items
C. number of frozen foods used on the menu
D. savings effected in purchasing in bulk at advantageous times

8. Before recommending a time-saving device, the MOST important factor to be considered is 8.____

A. whether it will be used frequently
B. the amount of maintenance which will be required
C. the number of productive labor hours which will be saved
D. the space it will require

9. Before planning a kitchen layout, it is MOST important to know 9.____

A. how much money will be available
B. the relation of the kitchen to other areas
C. the numbers and availability of personnel
D. what types of menus and service will be used

10. Kitchen equipment should be placed PRIMARILY to 10.____

A. provide neat, uncluttered appearance
B. avoid cross traffic
C. permit easy access to the main delivery area
D. establish a separate work area for each cook

11. The MAIN advantage of using standardized pans is that 11.____

A. the same pan can be used for cooking, serving, and storing
B. fewer pans are required
C. they stack better and require less storage space
D. less time is used to select the right pan for the job

12. Specific cleaning agents and detergents have been recommended for use on various 12.____
surface materials in order to do a thorough job of cleaning and to maintain the attractive
appearance of the material.
Of the following, the one which you would recommend for the purpose indicated is

A. tri-sodium phosphate for cleaning aluminum pots and pans
B. a scouring cleanser with a high percent of abrasive material for cleaning stainless
   steel tables and trucks
C. a lye base liquid soap for use in automatic dishwashing machines
D. a non-oil base detergent for floors covered with light-colored rubber tile

13. Scraping and prerinsing of dishes before running them through the dishwashing machine 13.____
is necessary to

A.   shorten the time of the washing process
B.   reduce the amount of detergent needed
C.   prevent blocking of the nozzles in the rinse arm of the machine
D.   remove food particles which harden at the wash temperature

14.   When purchasing food, the one of the following which should be the deciding factor for determining what is the MOST economical buy is the          14.____

A.   unit price as purchased
B.   cost of edible portion
C.   cost of product as served
D.   preparation costs

15.   When ordering perishable foods, the specification should designate the condition of the foods as of the time of          15.____

A.   delivery          B.   shipment          C.   packaging          D.   bidding

16.   Of the following forms in which meat can be purchased, the form which makes possible MOST accurate portion control is          16.____

A.   quarters                    B.   prefabricated
C.   carcass                     D.   wholesale cuts

17.   Fresh fruits are generally at their best during certain periods.
Of the following, the statement which is LEAST accurate is that          17.____

A.   cherries are best in June and July
B.   cranberries are best from April to September
C.   grapefruit is best from November to February
D.   California grapes are best from November to February

18.   When labor is the MOST important consideration, it is BEST to purchase potatoes          18.____

A.   whole, unpeeled              B.   whole, peeled
C.   instant, powdered            D.   canned

19.   When purchasing grapefruit for an institution, it is BEST to purchase by the          19.____

A.   pound          B.   dozen          C.   bushel          D.   crate count

20.   Of the following, the specification which is LEAST desirable when purchasing fresh vegetables is          20.____

A.   cauliflower, leaves trimmed to within 1" to 2" from head
B.   beets, stems completely removed
C.   carrots, topped, tops cut back to less than 1"
D.   celery, stalk length 16" and well trimmed

21.   When accepting a delivery of a large order of frozen foods, it is MOST important to          21.____

A.   be sure that the grade which was ordered is received
B.   see that the labels are intact
C.   check for evidence of defrosting
D.   weigh the merchandise to be sure of correct weight

22. For proper storage of dry and canned food supplies, it is NOT advisable to    22.____

    A.   place all shelving and stacks close against the wall to prevent falling
    B.   stack like items together to facilitate issuing and taking of inventories
    C.   store canned goods on shelves or on platforms 4 to 6" off the floor
    D.   stack the most recent receipts in back or on the bottom to make the *first in, first out* rule easy to follow

23. If a high bacteria count on the dishes is found in one of the serving units, it is LEAST    23.____
important to

    A.   check the wash and rinse temperature of the dishwashing machine
    B.   check the technique for scraping, prerinsing, washing, and rinsing dishes
    C.   inspect the serving unit, including all equipment, for cleanliness
    D.   arrange for a physical examination of every employee in the department

24. Rodent control is of prime importance in maintaining sanitary conditions.    24.____
The MOST effective way to eliminate rodents is by

    A.   providing regular visits of licensed exterminators
    B.   use of traps baited with food
    C.   cautious use of rat poisons
    D.   elimination of harborages

25. The recommended daily dietary allowance of protein for an aged man is MOST NEARLY    25.____
_____ gm. per kg. body weight.

    A.  .5          B.  1          C.  1.5          D.  2

―――――

# KEY (CORRECT ANSWERS)

| | | | |
|---|---|---|---|
| 1. | A | 11. | A |
| 2. | A | 12. | D |
| 3. | B | 13. | D |
| 4. | A | 14. | C |
| 5. | B | 15. | A |
| 6. | B | 16. | B |
| 7. | A | 17. | B |
| 8. | C | 18. | C |
| 9. | D | 19. | D |
| 10. | B | 20. | B |

| | |
|---|---|
| 21. | C |
| 22. | A |
| 23. | D |
| 24. | D |
| 25. | B |

―――――

# TEST 2

DIRECTIONS: Each question or incomplete statement is followed by several suggested answers or completions. Select the one that BEST answers the question or completes the statement. *PRINT THE LETTER OF THE CORRECT ANSWER IN THE SPACE AT THE RIGHT.*

1. The GREATEST amount of protein per unit of body weight is needed during    1.____

     A. childhood      B. infancy      C. adolescence      D. pregnancy

2. The thiamine needs of the individual are dependent upon the    2.____

     A. total caloric intake          B. body weight
     C. body height              D. age

3. Of the following foods, the BEST source of riboflavin is    3.____

     A. lean meat      B. egg      C. milk      D. orange

4. Of the following groups of foods, the one which contains the LARGEST number of alka-line-ash foods is    4.____

     A. milk, sugar, and starch
     B. milk, meat, and potatoes
     C. all fruits and vegetables
     D. most fruits, most vegetables, and milk

5. Of the following nutrients, the one which may reduce the amount of radioactive strontium 90 which may be deposited in the body is    5.____

     A. vitamin D            B. calcium
     C. oleic acid           D. ascorbic acid

6. If taken in massive doses over a period of time, the vitamin which may cause toxic effects is    6.____

     A. ascorbic acid        B. pantothenic acid
     C. vitamin $B_{12}$          D. vitamin A

7. The vitamin which contains cobalt is    7.____

     A. vitamin $B_{12}$          B. folic acid
     C. ascorbic acid        D. riboflavin

8. The term *niacin equivalents* refers to    8.____

     A. foods which have an equivalent niacin content
     B. the increase necessary when metabolism is accelerated
     C. the quantitative tryptophan-niacin relationship
     D. the minimum amount of niacin which will protect against symptoms of pellagra

9. The blood cholesterol level is MOST affected by    9.____

     A. body cholesterol synthesis        B. ingestion of egg yolks
     C. total dietary cholesterol intake      D. total fat intake

10. The calcium is unavailable because it forms an insoluble salt in combination with oxalic     10.___
acid in

   A.  collards        B.  carrots        C.  beets        D.  spinach

11. Following convalescence from gastric surgery, a relatively high proportion of patients     11.___
experience distressing symptoms after eating.
The diet prescription for this condition is USUALLY

   A.  high protein, high fat, low carbohydrate
   B.  high protein, low fat, low carbohydrate
   C.  high protein, high carbohydrate, low fat
   D.  low protein, low fat, high carbohydrate

12. An increase of high residue foods in the diet is indicated in cases of     12.___

   A.  spastic constipation        B.  ulcerative colitis
   C.  atonic constipation        D.  diverticulitis

13. The dietary treatment for diseases of the liver consists of     13.___

   A.  high protein, high carbohydrate, and moderate fat intake
   B.  moderate protein, low carbohydrate, and low fat intake
   C.  high protein, moderate carbohydrate, and moderate fat intake
   D.  moderate protein, high carbohydrate, and low fat intake

14. The diet USUALLY prescribed for persons with hyperchlorhydria is _____ diet.     14.___

   A.  100 mg. sodium        B.  low residue
   C.  low phosphorus        D.  low purine

15. In the treatment of phenylketonuria, the diet MUST be modified so that     15.___

   A.  all protein is eliminated from the diet
   B.  phenylalanine is completely eliminated from the diet until the child is 5 years old
   C.  the serum level of phenylalanine is maintained within normal limits
   D.  milk and milk products are the only foods eliminated from the diet

16. When signs of impending hepatic coma appear in a patient with advanced cirrhosis, the     16.___
diet MOST likely to be ordered is

   A.  low protein        B.  low carbohydrate
   C.  low caloric        D.  fat free

17. The one of the following menus which would be BEST to serve to an ulcer patient who     17.___
follows kosher food laws is

   A.  cream of pea soup, cream cheese sandwich, asparagus tips, custard, milk
   B.  cream of pea soup, chicken, mashed potatoes, diced carrots, canned pears, milk
   C.  tomato juice, beef pattie, baked potato with butter, peas, junket, milk
   D.  apple juice, creamed diced shrimp on rice, peas, canned peaches, milk

18. In the treatment of gout, the one of the following which MUST often be restricted because it may inhibit the excretion of uric acid is
    18.\_\_\_\_

    A. carbohydrate              B. fats
    C. fluids                     D. calcium

19. Of the following groups of foods, the one which may be indicated in a gluten-free diet is
    19.\_\_\_\_

    A. rye, barley, and macaroni
    B. crackers, spaghetti, and rice
    C. cream of wheat, cornstarch, and oats
    D. corn, potato, and rice

20. The one of the following which would NOT alleviate the symptoms of the dumping syndrome is
    20.\_\_\_\_

    A. small frequent feedings instead of large meals
    B. dry meals with fluids taken only between meals
    C. emphasis on concentrated forms of carbohydrates
    D. avoidance of chilled foods

21. The one of the following symptoms which is MOST indicative of riboflavin deficiency is
    21.\_\_\_\_

    A. poor wound healing
    B. fissures at the corners of the mouth
    C. bone deformities
    D. simple goiter

22. A preschool child who is allowed to drink as much as 2 quarts of milk daily to the exclusion of adequate amounts of solid foods is MOST likely to be deficient in
    22.\_\_\_\_

    A. protein        B. riboflavin        C. iron          D. vitamin A

23. The ketosis which occurs in uncontrolled diabetes is caused by the excessive oxidation of
    23.\_\_\_\_

    A. B-complex vitamins          B. fats
    C. carbohydrates             D. ascorbic acid

24. *Hidden hunger* may be the result of a diet lacking in sufficient amounts of
    24.\_\_\_\_

    A. foods high in cellulose        B. high calorie foods
    C. protein foods               D. protective foods

25. A possible result of protein deficiency is
    25.\_\_\_\_

    A. edema                B. heart disease
    C. gout                  D. sprue

# KEY (CORRECT ANSWERS)

| | | | | |
|---|---|---|---|---|
| 1. | B | | 11. | A |
| 2. | A | | 12. | C |
| 3. | C | | 13. | A |
| 4. | D | | 14. | B |
| 5. | B | | 15. | C |
| 6. | D | | 16. | A |
| 7. | A | | 17. | A |
| 8. | C | | 18. | B |
| 9. | A | | 19. | D |
| 10. | D | | 20. | C |

| | |
|---|---|
| 21. | B |
| 22. | C |
| 23. | B |
| 24. | D |
| 25. | A |

---

# TEST 3

DIRECTIONS: Each question or incomplete statement is followed by several suggested answers or completions. Select the one that BEST answers the question or completes the statement. *PRINT THE LETTER OF THE CORRECT ANSWER IN THE SPACE AT THE RIGHT.*

1. A negative nitrogen balance occurs when

    A. more nitrogen is being ingested than is excreted in the urine
    B. new tissue is being built in periods of rapid growth
    C. dietary protein intake is adequate for tissue synthesis
    D. the body's energy needs must be met from the body's stores of fat and the reserves of protein

1.\_\_\_\_

2. When planning a diet for an overweight adolescent girl, it is MOST important to consider that

    A. the chief problem is controlling the intake of candy and rich desserts
    B. overweight often disappears by the end of the adolescent period
    C. most problems of overweight are glandular in origin
    D. emotional and social problems are often related to the obesity

2.\_\_\_\_

3. If a patient with a long-term illness has anorexia, it is MOST important that

    A. he lie down for a half hour before each meal
    B. he be served his favorite foods first
    C. his nutritional requirements be met in spite of his lack of appetite
    D. he be allowed an alcoholic beverage as an appetite stimulant

3.\_\_\_\_

4. Assume that the bakers have been scheduled to be off duty on Saturday and Sunday. Under these circumstances, the MOST suitable one of the following combinations of desserts for Sunday is

    A. brownie a la mode for dinner; cheesecake (frozen) for supper
    B. apple pie a la mode for dinner; baked bread pudding for supper
    C. butterscotch pie for dinner; canned fruit cocktail with cookies for supper
    D. cherry jello with sliced bananas for dinner; Napoleons for supper

4.\_\_\_\_

5. To increase consumer satisfaction, it is recommended that whenever possible a choice of menu items be offered.
Of the following, the choice of menu items which is LEAST appropriate for use in a hospital cafeteria is

    A. stewed prunes or fresh frozen orange juice
    B. half grapefruit or canned applesauce
    C. sliced bananas or baked applies
    D. pineapple juice or grapefruit sections

5.\_\_\_\_

6. When preparing the menu, it is important to consider ease in serving, overall economy, and utilization of manpower and supplies.
Of the following menu items, the combination which is LEAST appropriate for a hospital menu is

   A. sliced tomato salad or head lettuce salad
   B. carrot and raisin salad or Waldorf salad
   C. coleslaw or celery and carrot sticks
   D. marinated sliced cucumbers or tossed salad greens

6._____

7. Of the following, the one which BEST illustrates the principles of good menu planning is

   A. beef stew, creamed diced potatoes, mixed vegetable salad, bread, butter, chilled fruit cup, coffee, tea or milk
   B. baked stuffed pork chop, mashed potatoes, buttered broccoli, spiced applesauce, bread, butter, raspberry sherbet with vanilla cookies, coffee, tea or milk
   C. French fried shrimp, baked potato, fried eggplant, lettuce salad with Thousand Islands dressing, bread, butter, sugared doughnuts, coffee, tea or milk
   D. cream of celery soup, baked filet of sole, steamed diced potatoes, buttered cauliflower, bread, butter, lemon sherbet, coffee, tea or milk

7._____

8. Assume that a disaster has occurred and you have no gas or electricity in your hospital but you have steam and hot water. The feeding census has doubled to 3000.
The BEST of the following menus to serve under these circumstances is:

   A. steamed frankfurters, Creole lima beans, pickle slices, bread or rolls, butter, mustard, sliced pineapple, boxed cookies, coffee and milk
   B. cold cuts, potato salad, sliced tomatoes, bread, butter, mustard, fresh apples, coffee, milk
   C. tomato juice, hamburgers on a bun, sliced onion, coleslaw, potato chips, canned applesauce, coffee, milk
   D. egg salad on lettuce, baked potato, bread, butter, hot cocoa, canned fruit cocktail

8._____

9. The timing of the cooking of fresh and frozen vegetables must be carefully planned into each day's operation if the final product is to be of top quality when it is served. When cooking vegetables in a steam kettle, the vegetables are added after the water comes to a boil and timing begins when the water reboils.
Of the following, the one which would NOT result in a top quality product is cooking of twenty pounds of

   A. fresh broccoli for 15 to 20 minutes
   B. frozen peas for 25 to 30 minutes
   C. fresh asparagus for 5 to 10 minutes
   D. frozen chopped spinach for 10 to 15 minutes

9._____

10. Advance preparation enables the dietary department to serve a variety of menu items not otherwise possible.
The one of the following items which may be prepared 12 to 24 hours in advance without loss in quality is

   A. Brown Betty
   C. potato salad
   B. stuffed pork chops
   D. spiced pears

10._____

11. When the butcher is instructed to process meat for beef stew, he should be instructed to use beef _____ and beef _____.    11._____

    A. chuck; neck            B. loin; chuck
    C. round; ribs            D. neck; loin

12. Of the following, the food items which are NOT interchangeable in recipes are    12._____

    A. chocolate with cocoa and fat
    B. fresh whole milk with non-fat dry milk solids and fat plus water
    C. baking powder with buttermilk and soda
    D. hard flour with soft flour and cornstarch

13. To produce the BEST medium white sauce, you should add for each cup of milk _____ of flour.    13._____

    A. 1 teaspoon            B. 2 tablespoons
    C. 1/4 cup              D. 8 tablespoons

14. The quality of food when served is greatly affected by the timing of preparation and cooking.    14._____
The one of the following which is MOST likely to be of acceptable quality when served is

    A. corn on the cob husked in the morning, refrigerated in plastic bags until 3:30, and cooked for 25 minutes at 4 P.M. for evening meal hour 4:30 to 6 P.M.
    B. hamburgers made from beef freshly ground at 7 A.M., seasoned, shaped and panned at 9 A.M., cooked in oven at 10:30 A.M., and distributed to all dining rooms at 11:30 for noon service until 1 P.M.
    C. baked potatoes, sorted and washed the day before, panned at 7 A.M., placed in hot oven to bake at 20 minute intervals starting at 10:30 A.M., removed at same intervals starting at 11:15 A.M., pierced and sent to dining rooms for service starting at 11:30 A.M.
    D. jelly omelet made by skillet method by cracking eggs early in morning, frying omelets at 10:30 A.M., spreading and folding jelly into them, cutting into standard portions, and placing them in a warm oven to hold for serving at 11:30 to 1 P.M.

15. Of the following, the LEAST important consideration in planning menus is the    15._____

    A. facilities and equipment available for food preparation
    B. ethnic and cultural food habits of patients
    C. per capita budgetary allowance
    D. method of food service to be used

16. In planning alternate choices of food items on a selective menu, it is MOST important to list alternatives which are of approximately the same    16._____

    A. cost per portion            B. food grouping
    C. degree of acceptability       D. color and texture

17. Many hospitals favor the use of cycle menus to improve their food service. However, cycle menus should NOT be used to    17._____

    A. simplify menu writing
    B. promote standardization of recipes and food production procedures

C. provide a fixed, unalterable menu pattern
D. help maintain better cost control

18. The one of the following which is LEAST useful in computing raw food costs for a given period is the 18.____

    A. inventory records of foods received and issued
    B. unit and total costs of foods used
    C. records of overhead and salaries
    D. record of meals served

19. The one of the following which has LEAST value in pre-costing a menu before it is served is the 19.____

    A. desired portion size of each item
    B. cost of the ingredients
    C. cost of labor
    D. estimated number of portions required

20. When planning menus, one should try to include items which are generally acceptable to as many individuals as possible to reduce leftovers. 20.____
Of the following, the food you should plan to use LEAST often in order to avoid excessive leftovers is

    A. chicken a la king    B. roast beef
    C. lettuce and tomato salad    D. chocolate layer cake

21. To maintain good standards of nutrition, the LARGEST percentage of the food dollar should be spent for 21.____

    A. cereal products    B. fruits and vegetables
    C. dairy products    D. meats

22. When giving diet instruction to a patient, the FIRST thing a dietitian should do is to 22.____

    A. explain the essentials of an adequate diet
    B. determine the amount of money available for food
    C. determine present and previous patterns of eating
    D. explain that a change in food habits will make the patient healthier

23. Assume that an older person asks for advice on how he can achieve greater enjoyment of meals and less distress after eating. 23.____
Of the following, the suggestion you should NOT make is that he eat

    A. a good breakfast to start the day
    B. four or five light meals instead of three heavier meals
    C. mostly cereal products since these are easiest to prepare and masticate
    D. the heaviest meal at noon rather than at night if sleeping is difficult

24. Of the following, the MOST desirable dinner menu for a geriatric patient who is on a regular diet is 24.____

    A. grilled frankfurters, baked beans, cole slaw, baked apple
    B. pot roast, noodles, carrot timbale, applesauce

C. fried chicken, mashed potatoes, rutabagas, cheese strudel

D. broiled fish, French fried potatoes, broccoli, cherry pie

25. Of the following menus, the one which is LEAST acceptable from the point of view of good menu planning for a patient on a regular diet is                                25.____

    A. roast lamb, mashed potatoes, buttered carrot rings, applesauce, bread and butter, cottage pudding with custard sauce, coffee, tea or milk

    B. simmered corned beef, parsley buttered potatoes, steamed cabbage wedge, horseradish and beet relish, bread and butter, fresh fruit cup, coffee, tea, milk

    C. Salisbury steak with mushroom gravy, French fried potatoes, sliced tomato salad on chicory, French dressing, vanilla ice cream, oatmeal cookie, coffee, tea, milk

    D. baked cured ham with mustard sauce, scalloped sweet potatoes with apples, cole slaw, bread and butter, Boston cream pie, coffee, tea, milk

-------

# KEY (CORRECT ANSWERS)

|     |   |     |   |
|-----|---|-----|---|
| 1.  | D | 11. | A |
| 2.  | D | 12. | D |
| 3.  | C | 13. | B |
| 4.  | A | 14. | C |
| 5.  | C | 15. | D |
| 6.  | B | 16. | B |
| 7.  | B | 17. | C |
| 8.  | A | 18. | C |
| 9.  | B | 19. | D |
| 10. | D | 20. | A |

| 21. | D |
|-----|---|
| 22. | C |
| 23. | C |
| 24. | B |
| 25. | A |

-------

# EXAMINATION SECTION
## TEST 1

DIRECTIONS:   Each question or incomplete statement is followed by several suggested answers or completions. Select the one that BEST answers the question or completes the statement. *PRINT THE LETTER OF THE CORRECT ANSWER IN THE SPACE AT THE RIGHT.*

1. The one of the following groups of garnishes or accompaniments which is MOST appropriate for the entree designated is

    A. boiled beef; horseradish sour cream sauce, mixed pickles, beet and onion relish, lemon wedge
    B. roast veal; cranberry sauce, fried apple ring, parsley, French fried onion ring
    C. broiled fish; lemon wedge, tartar sauce, chopped parsley, lemon butter
    D. hamburger; sliced onion, catsup, French fried onion rings, Hollandaise sauce

1._____

2. Assume that the following menu has been submitted: chicken fricasee, mashed potatoes, cauliflower, bread and butter, applesauce, coffee, tea, milk.
The CHIEF defect of this menu is that it is

    A. inadequate in protein content
    B. lacking in color and texture contrast
    C. improperly balanced as to nutrient content
    D. too high in calories

2._____

3. Assume that the following menu has been submitted for lunch: baked ham, pan browned parsnips, baked sweet potato, cornbread and butter, Apple Brown Betty with whipped topping.
This menu is NOT well-planned primarily because

    A. there are too many calories
    B. there are no vitamin C foods
    C. there is not enough variety in texture of the foods
    D. the workload is not well distributed for the kitchen's cooking equipment

3._____

4. If a patient on a diabetic diet dislikes milk, he may exchange the milk with one

    A. bread exchange, one meat exchange, and one fat exchange
    B. fruit exchange
    C. bread exchange, one beverage, and one fat exchange
    D. meat exchange and one fruit exchange

4._____

5. The one of the following foods which can be used by a diabetic patient as a substitute in a meat exchange is

    A. ice cream                 B. cheddar cheese
    C. lima beans              D. blackeye peas

5._____

6. Of the following foods, the one which should NOT be included in a clear liquid diet is

    A. milk                       B. fat-free broth
    C. fruit or vegetable juice       D. carbonated beverages

6._____

7. The one of the following which is permitted on a 500 mg. sodium diet is          7.____

   A.  cornflakes                          B.  rice krispies
   C.  puffed wheat                      D.  wheat flakes

8. The one of the following statements which is INCORRECT is that riboflavin          8.____

   A.  helps the cells utilize oxygen
   B.  helps keep vision clear
   C.  prevents cracking of mouth corners
   D.  helps the body absorb calcium

9. The one of the following which is NOT concerned with the digestion of fat is          9.____

   A.  cholecystokinin                 B.  lipase
   C.  bile                              D.  ptyalin

10. The diet which should be given to a patient who has chronic kidney disease with nitrogen retention is          10.____

   A.  high protein, low carbohydrate
   B.  low protein
   C.  low calcium, low phosphorus
   D.  low purine

11. The diet MOST likely to be ordered for the pernicious vomiting of pregnancy is          11.____

   A.  high carbohydrate, low fat
   B.  high carbohydrate, high fat, high protein
   C.  low carbohydrate, low fat, high protein
   D.  high protein, low sodium

12. In the treatment of hemorrhagic and nutritional anemias, the MOST important nutrients to stress are iron and          12.____

   A.  protein        B.  vitamin A        C.  iodine        D.  vitamin E

13. The USUAL diet for a patient with acute gallbladder is a _____ diet.          13.____

   A.  low fat                          B.  1000 mg. sodium
   C.  high protein                     D.  low cholesterol

14. Assume that a leukemia patient has difficulty swallowing the foods prescribed for her. In order to provide a diet which is nutritionally adequate, it is LEAST advisable to recommend          14.____

   A.  a liquid diet emphasizing high caloric liquids and protein supplements
   B.  nasal tube feeding in order to meet all nutritional requirements and to avoid the problem of swallowing
   C.  a diet on which the meat is minced and all fruits and vegetables are pureed
   D.  a diet similar to the one prescribed for her except that each item is pureed

15. The diet MOST likely to be prescribed for a patient who has renal stones is a(n) _____ diet.          15.____

   A.  elimination                     B.  low oxalate
   C.  low cholesterol                D.  high carbohydrate, low protein, low fat

16. A rice diet is USUALLY prescribed for patients who          16._____

    A. have high blood pressure
    B. have a food allergy
    C. are recovering from a gallbladder operation
    D. require a high caloric intake

17. Patients suffering severe burns are MOST likely to have          17._____

    A. loss of serum protein          B. steatorrhea
    C. polyneuritis          D. stomatitis

18. Of the following statements concerning phenylketonuria, the one that is NOT correct is          18._____
    that it

    A. is caused by an enzyme deficiency
    B. leads to mental retardation
    C. is treated by the restriction of carbohydrates
    D. must be detected in the first few months of life in order to be treated

19. During all periods of growth, vitamin D is essential for efficient absorption and utilization          19._____
    of

    A. calcium and potassium          B. potassium and iron
    C. magnesium and calcium          D. phosphorus and calcium

20. In the treatment of urinary calculi, the one of the following which will assist in maintaining          20._____
    an acid urine is

    A. cranberry juice          B. peas
    C. cabbage          D. corn oil

21. Of the following, the food containing the HIGHEST amount of thiamine per 100 gram por-          21._____
    tion is

    A. fresh green peas          B. fresh pork
    C. fresh spinach          D. ground beef

22. The one of the following foods which is the POOREST source of niacin per 100 gram          22._____
    portion is

    A. lean meats          B. peanuts
    C. whole grain cereals          D. green leafy vegetables

23. Of the following lists of foods, the one which will contribute MOST to the ascorbic acid          23._____
    content of a diet is

    A. potatoes, green peppers, raw cabbage
    B. enriched bread, pork, turnips
    C. whole wheat bread, potatoes, prunes
    D. apples, dates, plums

24. Of the following foods, the content of unsaturated fatty acids is GREATEST in          24._____

    A. butter          B. corn oil
    C. beef suet          D. lard

25. Of the following, the one with the LOWEST vitamin C content per 4 oz. portion is
_____ juice.                                                                      25.____

   A.  orange                                 B.  lemon
   C.  tomato                                 D.  grapefruit

---

# KEY (CORRECT ANSWERS)

| 1. | C | | 11. | A |
|---|---|---|---|---|
| 2. | B | | 12. | A |
| 3. | D | | 13. | A |
| 4. | A | | 14. | C |
| 5. | B | | 15. | B |
| 6. | A | | 16. | A |
| 7. | C | | 17. | A |
| 8. | D | | 18. | C |
| 9. | D | | 19. | D |
| 10. | B | | 20. | A |

| 21. | B |
|---|---|
| 22. | D |
| 23. | A |
| 24. | B |
| 25. | C |

---

# TEST 2

DIRECTIONS: Each question or incomplete statement is followed by several suggested answers or completions. Select the one that BEST answers the question or completes the statement. *PRINT THE LETTER OF THE CORRECT ANSWER IN THE SPACE AT THE RIGHT.*

1. When roasting meat, the GREATEST yield of finished product may be expected when      1.\_\_\_\_\_

    A.  it is quickly seared on both sides at the beginning
    B.  a high temperature is used throughout the roasting period
    C.  a small quantity of water is added during roasting
    D.  a low temperature is used throughout the roasting process

2. Of the following, the meat which is LEAST suitable for roasting is      2.\_\_\_\_\_

    A.  loin of pork                B.  corned brisket
    C.  rump of veal             D.  leg of lamb

3. The loss of weight which results from braising boneless bottom round of beef, when proper techniques are used, is      3.\_\_\_\_\_

    A.  negligible               B.  about 10%
    C.  about 25%             D.  over 50%

4. Of the following, the one which gives the MOST appropriate cooking temperature for the food indicated is      4.\_\_\_\_\_

    A.  beef loaf - 450° F         B.  baked potatoes - 250° F
    C.  caramel custard - 325° F     D.  gingerbread - 475° F

5. In teaching a *cook trainee* how to deep fat fry various items of food, one should NOT instruct him to      5.\_\_\_\_\_

    A.  lower the food into the fat quickly
    B.  make uniform portions of food for frying in the same load
    C.  fill frying baskets to no more than 2/3 of capacity
    D.  drain raw wet foods well before frying

6. Foods cooked incorrectly often lose flavor.
When cooking beans or carrots, it is LEAST advisable to      6.\_\_\_\_\_

    A.  boil them in a small amount of water
    B.  cook them in a steamer
    C.  cook them in a pressure cooker
    D.  cook them in an uncovered kettle

7. Of the following, the one which would make the LEAST satisfactory thickening agent in a casserole is      7.\_\_\_\_\_

    A.  wheat flour             B.  rice
    C.  cornstarch            D.  tapioca

8. If baking powder biscuits do not rise to the proper height, the MOST probable cause is too      8.\_\_\_\_\_

    A.  *little* shortening         B.  *much* handling of dough
    C.  *little* flour             D.  *much* baking powder

9. A soggy bottom crust in a lemon meringue pie is MOST probably caused by 9.___

    A. handling the crust too much
    B. baking at too high a temperature
    C. refrigeration of the crust prior to baking
    D. pouring in the filling when the pie is hot

10. The MOST appropriate type of poultry to purchase for chicken a la king is 10.___

    A. fowl    B. roasters    C. fryers    D. broilers

11. Of the following, Grade B eggs may be used MOST satisfactorily for 11.___

    A. poaching    B. scrambling
    C. frying    D. coddling

12. Considering both quality and economy, the BEST choice of the following grades to be specified when ordering apples for sauce is 12.___

    A. fancy    B. extra fancy
    C. utility    D. U.S. #1

13. When submitting requisitions, the dietitian should give correct specifications for each item.
Of the following items, the one which is CORRECTLY specified is 13.___

    A. celery - fresh, Grade A, trimmed, in boxes, 140 pounds
    B. oranges - fresh, commercial grade, size 75 to the half crate, 225 pounds
    C. salad greens - romaine, fresh, Grade A, trimmed, 30 pounds
    D. onions - dry, Grade A, in sacks, 200 pounds

14. The one of the following specifications which is INCOMPLETE is 14.___

    A. 200 lbs. of ham, 10 to 12 lbs. each, U.S. #1
    B. 120 lbs. fresh bottom rounds, 20 to 30 lbs. each, Choice
    C. 250 lbs. of boneless corned brisket, deckel removed, 10 to 12 lbs. each, Good
    D. 225 lbs. double veal legs, cut short, 40 to 48 lbs. each, Choice

15. Of the following food items, the one which does NOT have the correct varieties listed for it is 15.___

    A. melon - Honeydew, Cantaloupe, Persian, Casaba
    B. potatoes - Idaho, Cobbler, Russet, Yam
    C. onions - Spanish, Bermuda, Yellow, Red
    D. apples - McIntosh, Emperor, Delicious, Concord

16. Assume that you plan to serve 500 portions of beef stew, with 3 ounces of cooked meat in each portion.
To provide this, you would need _____ lbs. _____ beef chuck. 16.___

    A. 95; boneless    B. 100; whole
    C. 125; boneless    D. 175; whole

17. You are serving buttered carrot rings on a menu for which you need 750 servings. The number of pounds of topped carrots you should order is MOST NEARLY _____ lbs.

    A. 50          B. 75          C. 150          D. 300

17._____

18. Frozen broccoli is on the menu for dinner and you require 260 servings. The number of 2 1/2 lb. packages you would need is MOST NEARLY

    A. 10          B. 25          C. 50          D. 100

18._____

19. You wish to serve canned peas to 300 patients on the regular diet, 50 patients on bland diet, 35 patients on low fat diet, and 65 patients on light diet. Peas are supplied in #10 cans, and these are ordered by the case only.
The number of cases you would need is

    A. 1          B. 2          C. 3          D. 4

19._____

20. In order to ensure a minimum of leftover when you plan to serve 3 oz. portions of mashed potatoes to 500 persons, it would be BEST to order _____ potatoes.

    A. 40 lbs. instant
    B. 50 lbs. peeled
    C. 2 cases #10 cans of whole
    D. one 100 lb. sack of

20._____

21. The one of the following amounts which is MOST likely to yield 100 average servings is

    A. dry prunes, 25 lbs.
    B. bacon, sliced, rind removed (2 slices per serving), 20 lbs.
    C. coffee, ground for drip, percolator or silex, 2 lbs.
    D. egg noodles, buttered, 18 lbs.

21._____

22. The one of the following which would be INCORRECT to order when serving 200 persons is

    A. 8 #10 cans of applesauce
    B. 1 1/2 cases of #5 cans of tomato juice
    C. 100 lbs. of eviscerated fowl
    D. 20 lbs. of rice

22._____

23. To ensure that foods are relatively free of contamination when served in a cafeteria during a three hour meal period, it would be MOST advisable to

    A. stagger periods of preparation and service to the counter
    B. maintain a steam table temperature of 120° F
    C. reheat foods when they cool down
    D. eliminate all creamed foods from the menu

23._____

24. If egg salad has been prepared in a safe and sanitary manner, the criterion to be used to determine if it may be served one day later is that it

    A. still tastes good
    B. has a satisfactory general appearance
    C. still smells good
    D. has been continuously refrigerated

24._____

25. The one of the following statements concerning proper storage which is INCORRECT is    25.\_\_\_
    that

    A.  crates of eggs should be stored upright, never on ends or sides, because eggs are
        packed with the small end down
    B.  crates of lettuce or fruit should not be stacked upright but on the side and should
        be cross-stacked to provide for air circulation
    C.  fresh raw meat such as veal carcass should be carefully wrapped when stored to
        prevent contamination
    D.  onions and potatoes do not require refrigeration; they are best stored in a dark,
        well-ventilated room at a temperature of $50^\circ$ to $60^\circ$ F

─────────

# KEY (CORRECT ANSWERS)

| | | | |
|---|---|---|---|
| 1. | D | 11. | B |
| 2. | B | 12. | C |
| 3. | C | 13. | C |
| 4. | C | 14. | A |
| 5. | A | 15. | D |
| 6. | D | 16. | C |
| 7. | C | 17. | C |
| 8. | B | 18. | B |
| 9. | D | 19. | C |
| 10. | A | 20. | D |

| | |
|---|---|
| 21. | C |
| 22. | D |
| 23. | A |
| 24. | D |
| 25. | C |

─────────

# TEST 3

DIRECTIONS: Each question or incomplete statement is followed by several suggested answers or completions. Select the one that BEST answers the question or completes the statement. *PRINT THE LETTER OF THE CORRECT ANSWER IN THE SPACE AT THE RIGHT.*

1. Of the following, the one which gives the LEAST desirable temperature for storing the item indicated is

    1.____

  A.  ripe bananas - 60° to 70° F
  B.  fresh eggs - 53° to 58° F
  C.  salad greens - 40° to 45° F
  D.  fresh lamb - 33° to 38° F

2. Of the following, the MOST important reason for requiring good ventilation in a storeroom is to prevent

    2.____

  A.  condensation of moisture
  B.  roach or rodent infestation
  C.  complaints from storekeepers about odors
  D.  spoilage of canned goods

3. Of the following foods, the one which is LEAST susceptible to insect infestation is

    3.____

  A.  dried beans        B.  dried fruits
  C.  plain gelatin       D.  non-fat dry milk

4. Of the following, the MOST effective measure for the elimination of rodents in a hospital kitchen is to

    4.____

  A.  clean the floors every day
  B.  spread poison once a month in all allowable areas
  C.  eliminate harborages
  D.  screen off the slop sinks at all times

5. Of the following ways to store food, it is LEAST desirable to place

    5.____

  A.  sacks of dried beans on racks
  B.  cans of peas on the floor
  C.  packages of cereal on shelves
  D.  quarters of lamb on hooks in the refrigerator

6. The MOST important reason for NOT overcrowding refrigerators is to

    6.____

  A.  make cleaning easier
  B.  allow air circulation to reach all foods
  C.  prevent waste resulting from overlooked foods
  D.  reduce opportunities for pilferage of food

7. Cooked foods should be cooled and refrigerated quickly, PRIMARILY to

    7.____

  A.  *prevent* growth and development of bacteria
  B.  *preserve* food nutrients

C.   *prevent* loss of moisture content
D.   *preserve* a *fresh cooked* appearance

8.   In planning the layout of a kitchen, it is MOST important to arrange for       8._____

A.   grouping together of large pieces of equipment
B.   a separate work area for each cook
C.   a smooth and orderly flow of work
D.   separation of *wet* and *dry* areas

9.   Of the following, the MOST satisfactory work surface for a cook's work table is       9._____

A.   hardwood 4" thick
B.   heavy gauge stainless steel
C.   heavy duty galvanized iron
D.   heavy gauge aluminum

10.   Of the following, the practice which is LEAST advisable in the operation and mainte-       10._____
nance of a food grinder is to

A.   hold the knife and plate in place by screwing the adjustment ring as tight as possi-
ble
B.   use a mallet to push pieces of food into the grinder
C.   remove the grinder plate and clean it thoroughly with a brush after each use
D.   remove the grinder head at the end of the day and clean all loose parts before stor-
ing them

11.   The MAIN reason for selecting a cafeteria counter of standard fabricated units rather       11._____
than a custom-built counter of the same quality is the

A.   lower initial cost
B.   easier cleaning
C.   greater flexibility for change and expansion
D.   lower maintenance costs

12.   Of the following, the MOST suitable steam equipment for a main kitchen in a 100 bed       12._____
hospital is

A.   one compartment steamer, one 80 gallon jacketed kettle, and one 60 gallon jack-
eted kettle
B.   two 30 gallon jacketed kettles and one 20 gallon jacketed kettle
C.   one 3 compartment steamer and two 30 gallon jacketed kettles
D.   two 2 compartment steamers and one 20 gallon jacketed kettle

13.   The BEST choice for the top of a kitchen work table is       13._____

A.   2 inch solid wood
B.   12 gauge monel metal
C.   20 gauge stainless steel
D.   galvanized metal

14. For equipment such as steam tables which require a water supply, it is MOST important to    14.____

    A. make sure there are no submerged inlets
    B. specify all stainless steel construction
    C. provide a heat booster
    D. supply both hot and cold water

15. In requisitioning a steam jacketed kettle, the LEAST important specification is that the    15.____

    A. draw off tube should be as close to the kettle as possible
    B. bottom should be pitched to facilitate run-off of contents
    C. kettle should be wall hung for easier cleaning
    D. draw off valve should be easily removable

16. The MAIN factor to consider when purchasing a slicing machine is the    16.____

    A. ease of cleaning
    B. adequacy of the safety guard for the cutting edge
    C. size of the machine in relation to the volume of slicing
    D. availability of replacement parts

17. In submitting your annual budget, you have requested a 2 drawer work table of complete stainless steel construction.    17.____
If you are told that you must request a less expensive model, the MOST acceptable compromise for you to make would be to

    A. substitute ducoed legs with stainless steel feet
    B. substitute drawers of galvanized metal with stainless steel fronts
    C. specify a lighter weight stainless steel
    D. reduce the size of the table

18. The one of the following which is MOST likely to yield 100 average servings is    18.____

    A. fish filet - 30 pounds
    B. cream for coffee - 6 quarts
    C. oatmeal (rolled oats) - 5 pounds
    D. frozen spinach - 10 pounds

19. The one of the following requisitions which is NOT correct for 600 servings is    19.____

    A. 15 lbs. of ground coffee
    B. 9 lbs. of margarine chips for toast
    C. 3 #10 cans of jelly
    D. 60 lbs. of granulated sugar for cereal

20. You have requisitioned 8000 lbs. of beef carcass (650 to 700 lbs. per carcass). This will yield tender steaks, tender roasts, and less tender cuts for roasting, stewing, and chopping.    20.____
Taking into account loss from trim, bones, and fat when the carcasses are processed, the amount of edible meat these carcasses should yield is MOST NEARLY _____ lbs.

    A. 4500    B. 5360    C. 6500    D. 7120

21. Analysis of the distribution of the average food dollar in a hospital can be of assistance to the dietitian in planning for and checking on the expenditure of funds.
Of the following, the MOST advisable distribution of funds for categories of food is: meat, poultry, and fish _____%; dairy products _____%; fruits and vegetables _____%; bread and cereal _____%; miscellaneous _____%.

    A.  40; 20; 20; 10; 10                   B.  50; 10; 10; 10; 20
    C.  20; 20; 20; 20; 20                   D.  30; 30; 30; 5; 5

21.____

22. When planning a nutrition curriculum for the clinical instruction of student nurses, the factor which deserves the LEAST consideration is the

    A.  educational purposes which the school of nursing seeks to attain
    B.  educational experiences which are likely to meet the school's objectives
    C.  service needs of the dietary department of the hospital
    D.  methods of determining if the educational objectives have been attained

22.____

23. The current trend in the teaching of nutrition and diet therapy to student nurses emphasizes

    A.  role playing and discussion groups as the most significant teaching devices
    B.  instruction in food laboratories on preparation of foods
    C.  instruction in food preparation and service to patients in the wards
    D.  the clinical importance of diet therapy in a patient-centered plan of teaching

23.____

24. Suppose that the electric slicer used in the main kitchen is frequently out of order because of a short in the motor. The repair mechanic has demonstrated that this happens because excessive moisture is being used to flush out debris when cleaning the machine.
To prevent repetition of this breakdown, it would be MOST advisable to

    A.  issue detailed written instructions on maintenance procedures to all cooks and kitchen employees who might have occasion to use or clean this slicer
    B.  issue an order to all employees that no water is to
    C.  be used when cleaning this slicer, only clean dry rags
    D.  replace the slicer with a manual one that does not have a motor and, therefore, does not require electric current
    E.  instruct two employees on each shift on the procedures to be used in cleaning the machine and restrict the use of the machine to them

24.____

25. Assume that a dietitian had instructed the kitchen helpers on how to minimize waste when preparing food for cooking. It would be MOST reasonable to conclude that such waste had been reduced subsequently if

    A.  on a spot check, the employees observed were preparing the food as instructed
    B.  operating costs for the dietary division during the next month were reduced
    C.  the amount of food prepared during the next month decreased on a per capita basis
    D.  requisitions of food supplies during the next month decreased

25.____

# KEY (CORRECT ANSWERS)

| | | | |
|---|---|---|---|
| 1. | B | 11. | C |
| 2. | A | 12. | C |
| 3. | C | 13. | B |
| 4. | C | 14. | A |
| 5. | B | 15. | C |
| 6. | B | 16. | B |
| 7. | A | 17. | A |
| 8. | C | 18. | A |
| 9. | B | 19. | D |
| 10. | A | 20. | B |

| | |
|---|---|
| 21. | A |
| 22. | C |
| 23. | D |
| 24. | D |
| 25. | C |

# EXAMINATION SECTION
# TEST 1

DIRECTIONS: Each question or incomplete statement is followed by several suggested answers or completions. Select the one that BEST answers the question or completes the statement. *PRINT THE LETTER OF THE CORRECT ANSWER IN THE SPACE AT THE RIGHT.*

1. The one of the following which is the MOST important requirement of a good menu is that it

    A. include a large variety of food
    B. list foods which are well-liked
    C. be printed neatly on a clean menu card
    D. be suited to the purpose for which it is planned

1.\_\_\_\_

2. Of the following, the procedure which is MOST desirable for proper tray service is to

    A. heat all dishes before placing them on the tray
    B. serve hot food hot, and cold food cold
    C. have all patients elevated in order to permit easier swallowing of food
    D. always serve iced water on the tray

2.\_\_\_\_

3. The PROPER position for the knife on the tray is

    A. above the dinner plate
    B. across the bread and butter plate
    C. to the right of the dinner plate
    D. next to the fork

3.\_\_\_\_

4. For attractive tray service, it is MOST advisable to serve harvard beets

    A. on the plate with the meat
    B. in a small side vegetable dish
    C. on a bed of shredded lettuce
    D. with a very thick, heavy sauce

4.\_\_\_\_

5. The kitchen dietitian can work MOST efficiently if her office is located

    A. away from the kitchen, so she can be free from distractions
    B. in a central position where she may view all that happens
    C. at the entrance to the kitchen where she can see people entering and leaving
    D. next to the pantry, so she can see that no unauthorized person enters

5.\_\_\_\_

6. The PRIMARY purpose of keeping records in the dietary department is to

    A. reduce waste in ordering food and supplies
    B. increase consumption of the most nutritious foods
    C. train subordinates in office techniques
    D. maintain statistical records of retail prices

6.\_\_\_\_

7. A budget is BEST described as a(n)  7.___

    A. detailed plan for expenditures
    B. schedule for figuring depreciation of equipment over a period of years
    C. order for necessary equipment
    D. periodic accounting for past expenditures

8. Of the following, the CHIEF reason why a refrigerator door should NOT be left open is that the open door will  8.___

    A. stop the motor
    B. cause a drop in room temperature
    C. permit the cold air to rise to the top
    D. permit warm air to enter the refrigerator

9. Ovens with thermostatic heat controls should be  9.___

    A. kept closed at all times
    B. opened carefully to prevent jarring
    C. checked periodically for accuracy
    D. disconnected when not in use

10. The term *net weight* means MOST NEARLY the  10.___

    A. actual weight of an item
    B. weight of the container when empty
    C. combined weight of an item and its container
    D. estimated weight of the container alone

11. In requisitioning food, it is LEAST necessary for a dietitian to  11.___

    A. specify the exact quantity desired
    B. secure the signature of the cashier
    C. know the delivery times and order accordingly
    D. know the sizes in which foods are marketed

12. When receiving an order of food, it is INADVISABLE for the dietitian to  12.___

    A. check carefully against the order or requisition
    B. see that all fresh foods are weighed and checked in at the receiving room
    C. check for quality as well as quantity of foods delivered
    D. subtract two pounds tare from the weight of each package delivered in an order

13. Assume that, when inspecting a delivery of vegetables, you find a large amount of sorrel mixed in with a bushel of spinach.  13.___
The one of the following actions which it is MOST advisable for you to take is to

    A. sort the spinach and sorrel in cleaning and cook them separately to allow greater variety in the menu
    B. discard the sorrel as waste
    C. call the purchasing office and arrange to return the spinach as unsatisfactory
    D. place the sorrel in the refrigerator and return it to the driver on his next delivery

14. When purchasing iceberg lettuce, it is ADVISABLE to look for lettuce which is          14.____
    A.  loosely headed, with soft curly leaves and a yellow heart
    B.  tightly headed, elongated, with coarse green leaves
    C.  tightly headed, with medium green outside leaves and a pale green heart
    D.  loosely headed, with elongated stalk and rugged curly leaves

15. The term *30-40 prunes* is used to describe the          15.____
    A.  number of prunes in a box
    B.  particular variety of prunes
    C.  brand name of prunes
    D.  number of prunes in a pound

16. When ordering chocolate liquor, the dietitian should expect to receive a _____ choco-          16.____
late.
    A.  solid piece of        B.  semi-liquid
    C.  liquid              D.  glass jar of

17. Of the following, the BEST reason for discarding the green part of potatoes is that it con-          17.____
tains a poison known as
    A.  cevitamic acid        B.  citric acid
    C.  solanine            D.  trichinae

18. The number of cans that a standard case of #10 canned apples USUALLY contains is          18.____
    A.  6         B.  12        C.  18        D.  24

19. Of the following, the person MOST closely associated with work in the field of infant          19.____
behavior and feeding is
    A.  H. Pollack        B.  A. Gesell
    C.  E.J. Stieglitz      D.  J.F. Freeman

20. Of the following, the person BEST known for work in the field of diabetes is          20.____
    A.  N. Jolliffe        B.  H. Sherman
    C.  R.M. Wilder      D.  F. Stern

21. An egg which is strictly fresh will          21.____
    A.  float in cold water
    B.  have a thin and watery egg white
    C.  have a swollen egg yolk which is easily broken
    D.  sink in cold water

22. Cocoa and chocolate are rich in          22.____
    A.  glycogen     B.  gum      C.  cellulose     D.  starch

23. The percentage of protein that is usually converted into glucose in the body is MOST          23.____
NEARLY
    A.  49%      B.  58%      C.  67%      D.  78%

24. Of the following vegetables, the one which gives the LARGEST yield, pound for pound, when pureed is    24.___

    A.  fresh celery                  B.  frozen peas
    C.  frozen asparagus         D.  fresh carrots

25. If the composition of two small rib chops is Protein - 21 grams and Fat - 17 grams, the number of calories in the two chops is MOST NEARLY    25.___

    A.  136         B.  200         C.  237         D.  257

———

# KEY (CORRECT ANSWERS)

| | | | | |
|---|---|---|---|---|
| 1. | D | | 11. | B |
| 2. | B | | 12. | D |
| 3. | C | | 13. | C |
| 4. | B | | 14. | C |
| 5. | B | | 15. | D |
| 6. | A | | 16. | C |
| 7. | A | | 17. | C |
| 8. | D | | 18. | A |
| 9. | C | | 19. | B |
| 10. | A | | 20. | C |

| | |
|---|---|
| 21. | D |
| 22. | D |
| 23. | B |
| 24. | D |
| 25. | C |

———

# TEST 2

DIRECTIONS: Each question or incomplete statement is followed by several suggested answers or completions. Select the one that BEST answers the question or completes the statement. *PRINT THE LETTER OF THE CORRECT ANSWER IN THE SPACE AT THE RIGHT.*

1. An APPROPRIATE substitute for sucrose for a patient on a low carbohydrate diet is          1._____

   A. saccharin      B. casec          C. lactose          D. protinol

2. Of the following, the vegetables which are high in protein and, therefore, sometimes sub-          2._____
   stituted for meat are

   A. green leafy vegetables          B. legumes
   C. root vegetables                 D. gourds

3. When planning menus, it is *advisable* to use fish at least once a week because it is a          3._____
   GOOD source of

   A. iron          B. vitamin C          C. zinc          D. iodine

4. Of the following, the one which is a *non-nutritive* beverage is          4._____

   A. clear tea          B. orangeade
   C. oatmeal gruel      D. cream soda

5. Macaroni is *usually* used as a substitute for          5._____

   A. salad          B. meat          C. potato          D. dessert

6. Bread is dextrinized by          6._____

   A. toasting                B. chopping
   C. drying in open air      D. soaking in hot water

7. Baked custard is used on the menu CHIEFLY          7._____

   A. as a source of vitamin C
   B. because of its high protein content
   C. to add color
   D. as a source of starch

8. The one of the following which is a *non-irritating* food is          8._____

   A. cabbage      B. pickles          C. spaghetti          D. celery

9. Leaves of rhubarb and beets, when boiled in an aluminum container, will clean the con-          9._____
   tainer because they contain

   A. sulphuric acid          B. oxalic acid
   C. ammonia                 D. alkali

10. When refinishing a refrigerator ice cube tray, the one of the following which should NOT          10._____
    be used as a coating material is

    A. aluminum      B. cadmium          C. tin          D. nickel

11. The Department of Health requires the sterilization of eating utensils by        11.___

      A.  hot air sterilizers                   B.  ultraviolet rays
      C.  chemical solutions               D.  water at 180° F

12. Suppose that the dishwashing machine has become clogged with food particles.      12.___
Of the following, the action which would be MOST advisable for the dietitian to take
*first* is to

      A.  call the service man to disassemble and clean the machine
      B.  instruct the employees assigned to washing dishes about proper scraping of
          dishes
      C.  order the employees to prerinse all dishes in order to prevent clogging
      D.  remove the strainer tray

13. The one of the following which is the MOST effective way to rid a food storeroom of mice    13.___
is to

      A.  cement tight all holes which permit invasion
      B.  set traps to catch the mice
      C.  spread poison around the floor
      D.  burn a sulphur candle in the storeroom

14. Black stoves are cleaned BEST by                 14.___

      A.  polishing with an oiled cloth
      B.  rubbing with a piece of wax paper
      C.  scrubbing with soap and water
      D.  heating until they are red hot

15. Of the following, the BEST procedure for cleaning a red quarry tile floor in a hospital    15.___
kitchen is to

      A.  scrub it, then wax the floor
      B.  hose it down with steam
      C.  wash it with a strong soap
      D.  wash it with a lye

16. After making ice cream, it is MOST important that the machine be          16.___

      A.  rinsed thoroughly in cold water
      B.  sterilized
      C.  soaked in soap solution
      D.  scrubbed with a brush

17. A dietitian assigned to work with clinic patients should have a basic knowledge of the    17.___
foods of foreign-born people.
Of the following, the MOST important reason for this is that

      A.  it is interesting and exciting to eat the exotic dishes of foreign lands
      B.  such knowledge would prove beyond doubt that poor diet is the cause of poor
          health among the foreign-born

C. such knowledge would help the dietitian to plan the patient's prescribed diet around familiar foods
D. many foreign dishes are more nutritious than American foods

18. The clinic dietitian meets several problems of the aging. The one of the following for which she is LEAST responsible is the

    18._____

A. detection of the onset of chronic degenerative diseases
B. conservation of the health of the individual
C. re-evaluation of the caloric requirements of aged patients
D. overcoming of superstitions and food fallacies

19. When advising on methods of economizing, the clinic dietitian should instruct patients to AVOID buying

    19._____

A. foods in quantity, even though storage space permits
B. foods that are in season and in abundance on the market
C. less expensive cuts of meat
D. butter, since there are less expensive substitutes on the market

20. The one of the following services which is the LEAST basic function of a nutrition clinic is to

    20._____

A. serve as a teaching center for students
B. provide educational programs for patients of all ages
C. follow up the nutritional status of individual patients
D. secure diet histories of patients for the correction of undesirable food habits

21. Time and motion studies in the field of dietetics are used PRIMARILY to

    21._____

A. check on lateness and absence records of employees
B. reduce effort and increase efficiency in performing particular tasks
C. prepare estimates of time required between requisition and delivery dates
D. schedule the daily work assignments for the entire staff

22. The PRIMARY purpose of using standardized recipes is to

    22._____

A. aid in controlling food costs
B. encourage the cooks to try out new foods
C. prepare large quantities of food
D. determine the caloric values of foods

23. The CHIEF advantage of keeping a perpetual inventory of stock items is that

    23._____

A. supplies may be stored more easily
B. there will be less breakage and loss of stock
C. it makes it unnecessary to order replacements for stock supplies
D. the balance on hand at any time is easily determined

24. In order to prevent the loss of vitamins in cooking, it is HOST advisable to

    24._____

A. cover the food completely with water while cooking and boil it rapidly
B. peel and soak vegetables in cold water before cooking

C. dice vegetables into small pieces and boil them in an open pot
D. cook vegetables in the shortest possible time in a covered pot containing little water

25. To marinate is to                                                                                      25.___

A. let foods stand in a specially prepared liquid to add flavor or to tenderize them
B. cook food in liquid just below the boiling point
C. moisten food while cooking by pouring over it drippings or other liquids
D. cook food in water at boiling temperature

——————

# KEY (CORRECT ANSWERS)

| | | | |
|---|---|---|---|
| 1. A | | 11. D | |
| 2. B | | 12. A | |
| 3. D | | 13. A | |
| 4. A | | 14. C | |
| 5. C | | 15. B | |
| 6. A | | 16. B | |
| 7. B | | 17. C | |
| 8. C | | 18. A | |
| 9. B | | 19. D | |
| 10. B | | 20. A | |

21. B
22. A
23. D
24. D
25. A

——————

# EXAMINATION SECTION
## TEST 1

DIRECTIONS:   Each question or incomplete statement is followed by several suggested answers or completions. Select the one that BEST answers the question or completes the statement. *PRINT THE LETTER OF THE CORRECT ANSWER IN THE SPACE AT THE RIGHT.*

1. Foods which are left over may be used by the menu planner CHIEFLY to          1.____

   A.   baste meats
   B.   stock the freezer with emergency supplies
   C.   provide more variety in the next day's menu
   D.   add minerals to the diet

2. When a recipe calls for cooking in a hot oven, it is MOST desirable to set the thermostat          2.____
   at a Fahrenheit temperature of

   A.   300°          B.   350°          C.   425°          D.   525°

3. Of the following, the MOST satisfactory method for cooking the less tender cuts of meat          3.____
   is by

   A.   roasting          B.   broiling          C.   dry heat          D.   moist heat

4. A two-pound chicken is BEST prepared by          4.____

   A.   broiling          B.   stewing          C.   baking          D.   roasting

5. Fats are used in food preparation, *not only* as emulsifiers, *but also* as          5.____

   A.   shortening agents          B.   leavening agents
   C.   catalysts                  D.   sweetening agents

6. Baking powder is used in cake mixtures CHIEFLY in order to          6.____

   A.   improve the flavor
   B.   increase the acidity
   C.   lighten the cake and increase its volume
   D.   hold the other ingredients together

7. When making a sponge cake, it is important to remember to          7.____

   A.   beat the batter until it doubles in bulk
   B.   bake the cake in an ungreased tube pan
   C.   bake the cake in a hot oven
   D.   remove the cake from the pan as soon as it is baked

8. When making pastry, the fat should be          8.____

   A.   creamed with the flour
   B.   first melted and then creamed with the flour
   C.   cut into the flour
   D.   added to the flour after the water is stirred in

9. Of the following, the procedure which is MOST advisable when cooking dried prunes is to

    A. soak the fruit in hot water to seal in the juices
    B. keep the uncooked fruit under refrigeration at all times
    C. simmer the fruit slowly until it is tender
    D. add sugar to the fruit to improve the flavor

9.____

10. Assume that you plan to serve a gelatin dessert for dinner. You have found that gelatin made in the usual way softens in hot weather.
Of the following, the procedure which is MOST advisable to follow on a warm day is to

    A. thicken the gelatin with cornstarch
    B. substitute a non-gelatin dessert
    C. use fruit juice in the mixture
    D. use less water than usual

10.____

11. When preparing cream of tomato soup, it is MOST advisable to

    A. add hot milk slowly to cold tomato juice
    B. mix milk and tomato juice and then heat
    C. add cold tomato juice slowly to hot milk
    D. add cold milk slowly to hot tomato juice

11.____

12. In order to prevent cornstarch from lumping in cooking, it is MOST advisable to

    A. mix the starch with cold liquid before heating
    B. add hot liquid immediately to the starch
    C. brown the starch and add hot liquid
    D. heat the starch in a double boiler

12.____

13. Of the following, the LEAST desirable way to dry bread is to place it in

    A. uncovered pans on top of heated ovens
    B. paper bags which are suspended over the stoves
    C. deep pans in a warm oven
    D. cabinets which have slow heat

13.____

14. Of the following, the one which is a mollusk used in the preparation of soup is

    A. crab        B. oyster        C. lobster        D. cod

14.____

15. Whole dry milk is preferable to evaporated milk for use as a beverage CHIEFLY because it

    A. takes less time to prepare
    B. contains more vitamins
    C. can be made to look and taste more like whole milk
    D. contains more calories

15.____

16. The one of the following which is a RESIDUE-FREE food is

    A. milk                B. grapefruit sections
    C. lettuce           D. lemon gelatin

16.____

17. The one of the following which is NOT a legume is 17.____

    A. peanuts      B. okra      C. beans      D. lentils

18. Of the following, the sugar which is SWEETEST is 18.____

    A. lactose      B. fructose      C. sucrose      D. maltose

19. Broths are of value in the diet CHIEFLY because they are 19.____

    A. high in food value
    B. a good source of protein
    C. effective appetite stimulants
    D. a good source of carbohydrates

20. Of the following groups, the one which may be served on a SOFT diet is 20.____

    A. cream soup, mashed potato, spinach puree, toast, butter, custard
    B. broiled chicken, mashed potato, buttered peas, toast, milk
    C. vegetable soup, lamp chops, mashed potato, lettuce salad, toast
    D. clear broth, baked potato, tenderloin steak, carrots, apple pie

21. Of the following fruits, those which may be included in a HIGH ACID ash diet are 21.____

    A. prunes      B. oranges      C. bananas      D. pears

22. Of the following statements regarding yeast, the one which is MOST accurate is that yeast 22.____

    A. is generally harmful      B. changes starch to sugar
    C. lives without air      D. requires alcohol to live

23. The souring of milk is due PRIMARILY to the action of bacteria on 23.____

    A. fatty acids      B. proteins      C. amino acids      D. lactose

24. Glycerol, which is an end product of fat metabolism, is further oxidized in the body to 24.____

    A. sucrose      B. galactose      C. levulose      D. glucose

25. Cereals should be included in menus that are planned PRIMARILY to be 25.____

    A. weight reducing      B. low in starch
    C. low in cost      D. high in vitamin C

# KEY (CORRECT ANSWERS)

| | | | | |
|---|---|---|---|---|
| 1. | C | | 11. | C |
| 2. | C | | 12. | A |
| 3. | D | | 13. | A |
| 4. | A | | 14. | B |
| 5. | A | | 15. | C |
| 6. | C | | 16. | D |
| 7. | B | | 17. | B |
| 8. | C | | 18. | B |
| 9. | C | | 19. | C |
| 10. | D | | 20. | A |

| | |
|---|---|
| 21. | A |
| 22. | B |
| 23. | D |
| 24. | D |
| 25. | C |

---

# TEST 2

DIRECTIONS:  Each question or incomplete statement is followed by several suggested answers or completions. Select the one that BEST answers the question or completes the statement. *PRINT THE LETTER OF THE CORRECT ANSWER IN THE SPACE AT THE RIGHT.*

1. Of the following, a high blood sugar content is MOST likely to be a symptom of          1.____

    A.  anemia
    C.  arteriosclerosis
    B.  diabetes mellitus
    D.  hypertension

2. Trichinosis is a disease which may be caused by          2.____

    A.  eating ham which has been overcooked
    B.  unsanitary handling of frozen meats
    C.  eating food which has been contaminated by infected flies
    D.  eating infected pork which has been cooked insufficiently

3. Of the following, the bacteria which causes MOST food poisoning cases is          3.____

    A.  botulinum    B.  salmonella    C.  pneumococci    D.  streptococci

4. In the normal diet, liver should be used at least once a week since it is a GOOD source of          4.____

    A.  vitamin C    B.  phosphorus    C.  iron    D.  roughage

5. Water is important in the daily intake of the body CHIEFLY because it          5.____

    A.  causes the oxidation of food in the body
    B.  is a transporting medium for all body substances
    C.  cools the air in the lungs
    D.  gives off minerals when it is digested

6. Cod liver oil is given to children CHIEFLY in order to aid in          6.____

    A.  absorption of calcium
    C.  prevention of beriberi
    B.  carbohydrate metabolism
    D.  regulation of osmotic pressure

7. Of the following statements with respect to the nutritional needs of children, the one which is MOST accurate is that          7.____

    A.  a child of four years of age requires a minimum of 2000 calories a day
    B.  it is better for a child to be slightly underweight than to be overweight
    C.  proportionately, children require more protein per pound of body weight than do adults
    D.  a child whose diet is deficient in vitamin D may develop scurvy as a result

8. The one of the following desserts which it is MOST advisable to use in a low protein diet is          8.____

    A.  rune soufflé
    C.  gelatin
    B.  fruit cup
    D.  junket

9. The Karell diet is used in the care of                                                    9.___

    A. Addison's disease           B. cardiac conditions
    C. diabetes                   D. jaundice

10. Rowe elimination diets are used in cases involving                                        10.___

    A. allergy                  B. lead poisoning
    C. constipation            D. nephritis

11. Of the following conditions, the one for which the normal diet is MODIFIED by restricting sodium is                                                                          11.___

    A. tuberculosis    B. diabetes    C. gastritis    D. edema

12. The one of the following conditions which may cause jaundice is                           12.___

    A. faulty functioning of the kidneys
    B. an obstruction in the common bile duct
    C. a deficiency of vitamin C
    D. the presence of the yeast spore

13. It is GENERALLY accepted that exophthalmic goiter may result from                         13.___

    A. the inability of the body to metabolize purines
    B. injury to the pancreas
    C. a diet deficient in iodine
    D. lack of sufficient sunlight and milk

14. Faulty ossification of the legs, ribs, and cranial bones are symptoms GENERALLY associated with                                                                            14.___

    A. pellagra    B. rickets    C. neuritis    D. encephalitis

15. Of the following diseases, the one which is characterized PRIMARILY by destruction of the liver cells is                                                                    15.___

    A. diabetes    B. leukemia    C. scurvy    D. cirrhosis

Questions 16-25.

DIRECTIONS:   Column I lists 10 diseases or conditions, numbered 16 to 25, which require dietary treatment. Column II lists the dietary treatments which are generally used for the conditions listed in Column I. In the space at the right, opposite the number preceding each of the conditions in Column I, place the letter preceding the dietary treatment in Column II which is MOST appropriate for the condition in Column I.

| COLUMN I | COLUMN II | |
|---|---|---|
| 16. Addison's disease | A. low carbohydrate diet | 16. _____ |
| 17. cirrhosis | B. high caloric, non-stimulating diet | 17. _____ |
| 18. diabetes | C. non-residue diet, high in protein and acid ash | 18. _____ |
| 19. exophthalmic goiter | | 19. _____ |
| 20. gastric ulcer | D. diet high in vitamin C and mag-nesium | 20. _____ |
| 21. gout | E. high protein, high carbohydrate, low roughage diet | 21. _____ |
| 22. lipoid nephrosis | | 22. _____ |
| 23. obesity | F. high caloric, soft diet, given in small, frequent feedings | 23. _____ |
| 24. rickets | G. diet high in carbohydrate and vitamins, low in potassium, with added salt | 24. _____ |
| 25. typhoid fever | | 25. _____ |

H. diet with normal or high protein, vitamins, and minerals; low in fat and carbohydrate; low in caloric value

I. high protein and sulphur diet

J. low protein, purine-free diet

K. high protein, low fat diet, with lim-ited sodium

L. diet high in protein and carbohy-drate, low in fat, high in vitamin B complex

M. diet high in vitamin D

# KEY (CORRECT ANSWERS)

| | | | | |
|---|---|---|---|---|
| 1. | B | | 11. | D |
| 2. | D | | 12. | B |
| 3. | B | | 13. | C |
| 4. | C | | 14. | B |
| 5. | B | | 15. | D |
| | | | | |
| 6. | A | | 16. | G |
| 7. | C | | 17. | L |
| 8. | B | | 18. | A |
| 9. | B | | 19. | B |
| 10. | A | | 20. | F |

| | |
|---|---|
| 21. | J |
| 22. | K |
| 23. | H |
| 24. | M |
| 25. | E |

———

# RECORD KEEPING
## EXAMINATION SECTION
### TEST 1

DIRECTIONS: Each question or incomplete statement is followed by several suggested answers or completions. Select the one that BEST answers the question or completes the statement. *PRINT THE LETTER OF THE CORRECT ANSWER IN THE SPACE AT THE RIGHT.*

Questions 1-7.

DIRECTIONS: In answering Questions 1 through 7, use the following master list. For each question, determine where the name would fit on the master list. Each answer choice indicates right before or after the name in the answer choice.

Aaron, Jane
Armstead, Brendan
Bailey, Charles
Dent, Ricardo
Grant, Mark
Mars, Justin
Methieu, Justine
Parker, Cathy
Sampson, Suzy
Thomas, Heather

1. Schmidt, William
   A. Right before Cathy Parker
   B. Right after Heather Thomas
   C. Right after Suzy Sampson
   D. Right before Ricardo Dent

   1.____

2. Asanti, Kendall
   A. Right before Jane Aaron
   B. Right after Charles Bailey
   C. Right before Justine Methieu
   D. Right after Brendan Armstead

   2.____

3. O'Brien, Daniel
   A. Right after Justine Methieu
   B. Right before Jane Aaron
   C. Right after Mark Grant
   D. Right before Suzy Sampson

   3.____

4. Marrow, Alison
   A. Right before Cathy Parker
   B. Right before Justin Mars
   C. Right after Mark Grant
   D. Right after Heather Thomas

   4.____

5. Grantt, Marissa
   A. Right before Mark Grant
   B. Right after Mark Grant
   C. Right after Justin Mars
   D. Right before Suzy Sampson

   5.____

6.  Thompson, Heath                                                                              6.____
    A.  Right after Justin Mars          B.  Right before Suzy Sampson
    C.  Right after Heather Thomas       D.  Right before Cathy Parker

DIRECTIONS:  Before answering Question 7, add in all of the names from Questions 1 through
             6.  Then fit the name in alphabetical order based on the new list.

7.  Francisco, Mildred                                                                           7.____
    A.  Right before Mark Grant          B.  Right after Marissa Grantt
    C.  Right before Alison Marrow       D.  Right after Kendall Asanti

Questions 8-10.

DIRECTIONS:  In answering Questions 8 through 10, compare each pair of names and
             addresses.  Indicate whether they are the same or different in any way.

8.  William H. Pratt, J.D.              William H. Pratt, J.D.                                   8.____
    Attourney at Law                    Attorney at Law
    A.  No differences                  B.  1 difference
    C.  2 differences                   D.  3 differences

9.  1303 Theater Drive,; Apt. 3-B       1330 Theatre Drive,; Apt. 3-B                            9.____
    A.  No differences                  B.  1 difference
    C.  2 differences                   D.  3 differences

10. Petersdorff, Briana and Mary        Petersdorff, Briana and Mary                             10.____
    A.  No differences                  B.  1 difference
    C.  2 differences                   D.  3 differences

11. Which of the following words, if any, are misspelled?                                        11.____
    A.  Affordable                      B.  Circumstansial
    C.  Legalese                        D.  None of the above

Questions 12-13.

DIRECTIONS:  Questions 12 and 13 are to be answered on the basis of the following table.

Standardized Test Results for High School Students in District #1230

|                | English | Math | Science | Reading |
|----------------|---------|------|---------|---------|
| High School 1  | 21      | 22   | 15      | 18      |
| High School 2  | 12      | 16   | 13      | 15      |
| High School 3  | 16      | 181  | 21      | 17      |
| High School 4  | 19      | 14   | 15      | 16      |

The scores for each high school in the district were averaged out and listed for each
subject tested.  Scores of 0-10 are significantly below College Readiness Standards.  11-15 are
below College Readiness, 16-20 meet College Readiness, and 21-25 are above College
Readiness.

12. If the high schools need to meet or exceed in at least half the categories    12.____
in order to NOT be considered "at risk," which schools are considered "at risk"?
    A. High School 2             B. High School 3
    C. High School 4             D. Both A and C

13. What percentage of subjects did the district as a whole meet or exceed    13.____
College Readiness standards?
    A. 25%         B. 50%         C. 75%         D. 100%

Questions 14-15.

DIRECTIONS:   Questions 14 and 15 are to be answered on the basis of the following information.

You have seven employees working as a part of your team: Austin, Emily, Jeremy, Christina, Martin, Harriet, and Steve. You have just sent an e-mail informing them that there will be a mandatory training session next week. To ensure that work still gets done, you are offering the training twice during the week: once on Tuesday and also on Thursday. This way half the employees will still be working while the other half attend the training. The only other issue is that Jeremy doesn't work on Tuesdays and Harriet doesn't work on Thursdays due to compressed work schedules.

14. Which of the following is a possible attendance roster for the first training    14.____
session?
    A. Emily, Jeremy, Steve         B. Steve, Christina, Harriet
    C. Harriet, Jeremy, Austin       D. Steve, Martin, Jeremy

15. If Harriet, Christina, and Steve attend the training session on Tuesday, which    15.____
of the following is a possible roster for Thursday's training session?
    A. Jeremy, Emily, and Austin      B. Emily, Martin, and Harriet
    C. Austin, Christina, and Emily    D. Jeremy, Emily, and Steve

Questions 16-20.

DIRECTIONS:   In answering Questions 16 through 20, you will be given a word and will need to choose the answer choice that is MOST similar or different to the word.

16. Which word means the SAME as *annual*?    16.____
    A. Monthly        B. Usually        C. Yearly       D. Constantly

17. Which word means the SAME as *effort*?    17.____
    A. Energy        B. Equate        C. Cherish       D. Commence

18. Which word means the OPPOSITE of *forlorn*?    18.____
    A. Neglected      B. Lethargy      C. Optimistic     D. Astonished

19. Which word means the SAME as *risk*?    19.____
    A. Admire       B. Hazard      C. Limit       D. Hesitant

20. Which word means the OPPOSITE of *translucent*?
    A. Opaque         B. Transparent  C. Luminous     D. Introverted

20.____

21. Last year, Jamie's annual salary was $50,000. Her boss called her today to inform her that she would receive a 20% raise for the upcoming year. How much more money will Jamie receive next year?
    A. $60,000       B. $10,000     C. $1,000      D. $51,000

21.____

22. You and a co-worker work for a temp hiring agency as part of their office staff. You both are given 6 days off per month. How many days off are you and your co-worker given in a year?
    A. 24          B. 72         C. 144       D. 48

22.____

23. If Margot makes $34,000 per year and she works 40 hours per week for all 52 weeks, what is her hourly rate?
    A. $16.34/hour    B. $17.00/hour  C. $15.54/hour  D. $13.23/hour

23.____

24. How many dimes are there in $175.00?
    A. 175         B. 1,750      C. 3,500      D. 17,500

24.____

25. If Janey is three times as old as Emily, and Emily is 3, how old is Janey?
    A. 6         B. 9         C. 12       D. 15

25.____

# KEY (CORRECT ANSWERS)

| | | | | |
|---|---|---|---|---|
| 1. | C | | 11. | B |
| 2. | D | | 12. | A |
| 3. | A | | 13. | D |
| 4. | B | | 14. | B |
| 5. | B | | 15. | A |
| 6. | C | | 16. | C |
| 7. | A | | 17. | A |
| 8. | B | | 18. | C |
| 9. | C | | 19. | B |
| 10. | A | | 20. | A |

| | |
|---|---|
| 21. | B |
| 22. | C |
| 23. | A |
| 24. | B |
| 25. | B |

# TEST 2

DIRECTIONS: Each question or incomplete statement is followed by several suggested answers or completions. Select the one that BEST answers the question or completes the statement. *PRINT THE LETTER OF THE CORRECT ANSWER IN THE SPACE AT THE RIGHT.*

Questions 1-6.

DIRECTIONS: Questions 1 through 6 are to be answered on the basis of the following information.

| | |
|---|---|
| item | name of item to be ordered |
| quantity | minimum number that can be ordered |
| beginning amount | amount in stock at start of month |
| amount received | amount receiving during month |
| ending amount | amount in stock at end of month |
| amount used | amount used during month |
| amount to order | will need at least as much of each item as used in the previous month |
| unit price | cost of each unit of an item |
| total price | total price for the order |

| Item | Quantity | Beginning | Received | Ending | Amount Used | Amount to Order | Unit Price | Total Price |
|---|---|---|---|---|---|---|---|---|
| Pens | 10 | 22 | 10 | 8 | 24 | 20 | $0.11 | $2.20 |
| Spiral notebooks | 8 | 30 | 13 | 12 | | | $0.25 | |
| Binder clips | 2 boxes | 3 boxes | 1 box | 1 box | | | $1.79 | |
| Sticky notes | 3 packs | 12 packs | 4 packs | 2 packs | | | $14.29 | |
| Dry erase markers | 1 pack (dozen) | 34 markers | 8 markers | 40 markers | | | $16.49 | |
| Ink cartridges (printer) | 1 cartridge | 3 cartridges | 1 cartridge | 2 cartridges | | | $79.99 | |
| Folders | 10 folders | 25 folders | 15 folders | 10 folders | | | $1.08 | |

1. How many packs of sticky notes were used during the month?                1.____
   A. 16           B. 10           C. 12           D. 14

2. How many folders need to be ordered for next month?                2.____
   A. 15           B. 20           C. 30           D. 40

3. What is the total price of notebooks that you will need to order?                3.____
   A. $6.00           B. $0.25           C. $4.50           D. $2.75

4. Which of the following will you spend the second most money on?                4.____
   A. Ink cartridges           B. Dry erase markers
   C. Sticky notes           D. Binder clips

5. How many packs of dry erase markers should you order?                5.____
   A. 1           B. 8           C. 12           D. 0

6. What will be the total price of the file folders you order?        6._____
     A. $20.16      B. $2.16      C. $1.08      D. $4.32

Questions 7-11.

DIRECTIONS: Questions 7 through 11 are to be answered on the basis of the following table.

| Number of Car Accidents, By Location and Cause, for 2014 | | | | | | |
|---|---|---|---|---|---|---|
| | Location 1 | | Location 2 | | Location 3 | |
| Cause | Number | Percent | Number | Percent | Number | Percent |
| Severe Weather | 10 | | 25 | | 30 | |
| Excessive Speeding | 20 | 40 | 5 | | 10 | |
| Impaired Driving | 15 | | 15 | 25 | 8 | |
| Miscellaneous | 5 | | 15 | | 2 | 4 |
| TOTALS | 50 | 100 | 60 | 100 | 50 | 100 |

7. Which of the following is the third highest cause of accidents for all three     7._____
    locations?
     A. Severe Weather             B. Impaired Driving
     C. Miscellaneous             D. Excessive Speeding

8. The average number of Severe Weather accidents per week at Location 3     8._____
    for the year (52 weeks) was MOST NEARLY
     A. 0.57      B. 30      C. 1      D. 1.25

9. Which location had the LARGEST percentage of accidents caused by     9._____
    Impaired Driving?
     A. 1      B. 2      C. 3      D. Both A and B

10. If one-third of the accidents at all three locations resulted in at least one     10._____
     fatality, what is the LEAST amount of deaths caused by accidents last year?
     A. 60      B. 106      C. 66      D. 53

11. What is the percentage of accidents caused by miscellaneous means from     11._____
     all three locations in 2014?
     A. 5%      B. 10%      C. 13%      D. 25%

12. How many pairs of the following groups of letters are exactly alike?     12._____
      ACDOBJ           ACDBOJ
      HEWBWR          HEWRWB
      DEERVS           DEERVS
      BRFQSX           BRFQSX
      WEYRVB         WEYRVB
      SPQRZA          SQRPZA

     A. 2      B. 3      C. 4      D. 5

Questions 13-19.

DIRECTIONS: Questions 13 through 19 are to be answered on the basis of the following information.

In 2012, the most current information on the American population was finished. The population was compiled by 200 people from each of the 50 states. The territory of Puerto Rico, a sovereign of the United States, had 25 people assigned to compile data. In February of 2010, each state began collecting information. In Puerto Rico, data collection finished by January 31st, 2011, while the United States finished on June 30, 2012. Each volunteer gathered data on the population of each state or sovereign. When the information was compiled, each volunteer had to send their information to the nation's capital, Washington, D.C. Each worker worked 20 hours per month and put together 10 reports per month. After the data was compiled in total, 50 people reviewed the data and worked from January 2012 to December 2012.

13. How many reports were generated from February 2010 to April 2010 in Illinois and Ohio?
    A. 3,000        B. 6,000        C. 12,000        D. 15,000    13.____

14. How many workers in total were collecting data in January 2012?
    A. 200        B. 25        C. 225        D. 0    14.____

15. How many reports were put together in May 2012?
    A. 2,000        B. 50,000        C. 100,000        D. 100,250    15.____

16. How many hours did the Puerto Rican volunteers work in the fall (September-November)?
    A. 60        B. 500        C. 1,500        D. 0    16.____

17. How many workers were there in February 2011?
    A. 25        B. 200        C. 225        D. 250    17.____

18. What was the total amount of hours worked in July 2010?
    A. 500        B. 4,000        C. 4,500        D. 5,000    18.____

19. How many reviewers worked in January 2013?
    A. 75        B. 50        C. 0        D. 25    19.____

20. John has to file 10 documents per shelf. How many documents would it take for John to fill 40 shelves?
    A. 40        B. 400        C. 4,500        D. 5,000    20.____

21. Jill wants to travel from New York City to Los Angeles by bike, which is approximately 2,772 miles. How many miles per day would Jill need to average if she wanted to complete the trip in 4 weeks?
    A. 100        B. 89        C. 99        D. 94    21.____

22. If there are 24 CPU's and only 7 monitors, how many more monitors do
you need to have the same amount of monitors as CPU's?
    A.  Not enough information        B.  17
    C.  31        D.  0

22.____

23. If Gerry works 5 days a week and 8 hours each day, and John works 3 days
a week and 10 hours each day, how many more hours per year will Gerry work
than John?
    A.  They work the same amount of hours.
    B.  450
    C.  520
    D.  832

23.____

24. Jimmy gets transferred to a new office.  The new office has 25 employees,
but only 16 are there due to a blizzard.  How many coworkers was Jimmy able
to meet on his first day?
    A.  16        B.  25        C.  9        D.  7

24.____

25. If you do a fundraiser for charities in your area and raise $500 total, how
much would you give to each charity if you were donating equal amounts to 3
of them?
    A.  $250.00        B.  $167.77        C.  $50.00        D.  $111.11

25.____

# KEY (CORRECT ANSWERS)

| | | | | |
|---|---|---|---|---|
| 1. | D | | 11. | C |
| 2. | B | | 12. | B |
| 3. | A | | 13. | C |
| 4. | C | | 14. | A |
| 5. | D | | 15. | A |
| 6. | B | | 16. | C |
| 7. | D | | 17. | B |
| 8. | A | | 18. | C |
| 9. | A | | 19. | C |
| 10. | D | | 20. | B |

| | |
|---|---|
| 21. | C |
| 22. | B |
| 23. | C |
| 24. | A |
| 25. | B |

# TEST 3

DIRECTIONS: Each question or incomplete statement is followed by several suggested answers or completions. Select the one that BEST answers the question or completes the statement. *PRINT THE LETTER OF THE CORRECT ANSWER IN THE SPACE AT THE RIGHT.*

Questions 1-3.

DIRECTIONS: In answering Questions 1 through 3, choose the correctly spelled word.

1. A. allusion          B. alusion          C. allusien          D. allution          1.____

2. A. altitude          B. alltitude          C. atlitude          D. altlitude          2.____

3. A. althogh          B. allthough          C. althrough          D. although          3.____

Questions 4-9.

DIRECTIONS: In answering Questions 4 through 9, choose the answer that BEST completes the analogy.

4. Odometer is to mileage as compass is to          4.____
   A. speed          B. needle          C. hiking          D. direction

5. Marathon is to race as hibernation is to          5.____
   A. winter          B. dream          C. sleep          D. bear

6. Cup is to coffee as bowl is to          6.____
   A. dish          B. spoon          C. food          D. soup

7. Flow is to river as stagnant is to          7.____
   A. pool          B. rain          C. stream          D. canal

8. paw is to cat as hoof is to          8.____
   A. lamb          B. horse          C. lion          D. elephant

9. Architect is to building as sculptor is to          9.____
   A. museum          B. chisel          C. stone          D. statue

Questions 10-14.

DIRECTIONS:   Questions 10 through 14 are to be answered on the basis of the following
graph.

| Population of Carroll City Broken Down by Age and Gender | | | |
|---|---|---|---|
| (In Thousands) Age | Female | Male | Total |
| Under 15 | 60 | 60 | 80 |
| 15-23 | | 22 | |
| 24-33 | | 20 | 44 |
| 34-43 | 13 | 18 | 31 |
| 44-53 | 20 | | 67 |
| 64 and Over | 65 | 65 | 130 |
| TOTAL | 225 | 237 | 422 |

10.  How many people in the city are between the ages of 15-23?            10._____
    A.  70              B.  46,000        C.  70,000       D.  225,000

11.  Approximately what percentage of the total population of the city was       11._____
    female aged 24-33?
    A.  10%            B.  5%            C.  15%           D.  25%

12.  If 33% of the males have a job and 55% of females don't have a job,       12._____
    which of the following statements is TRUE?
    A.  Males have 2,251 more jobs than females.
    B.  Females have 44,760 more jobs than males.
    C.  Females have 22,251 more jobs than males.
    D.  None of the above statements are true.

13.  How many females between the ages of 15-23 live in Carroll City?        13._____
    A.  67,000          B.  24,000        C.  48,000       D.  91,000

14.  Assume all males 44-53 living in Carroll city are employed.  If two-thirds      14._____
    of males age 44-53 work jobs outside of Carroll City, how many work within city
    limits?
    A.  31,333
    B.  15,667
    C.  47,000
    D.  Cannot answer the question with the information provided

Questions 15-16.

DIRECTIONS:  Questions 15 and 16 are labeled as shown.  Alphabetize them for filing.
Choose the answer that correctly shows the order.

15.  (1)  AED                                                                                                    15._____
     (2)  OOS
     (3)  FOA
     (4)  DOM
     (5)  COB

      A.  2-5-4-3-2          B.  1-4-5-2-3          C.  1-5-4-2-3          D.  1-5-4-3-2

16.  Alphabetize the names of the people.  Last names are given last.               16._____
     (1)  Lindsey Jamestown
     (2)  Jane Alberta
     (3)  Ally Jamestown
     (4)  Allison Johnston
     (5)  Lyle Moreno

      A.  2-1-3-4-5          B.  3-4-2-1-5          C.  2-3-1-4-5          D.  4-3-2-1-5

17.  Which of the following words is misspelled?                                       17._____
     A.  disgust                          B.  whisper
     C.  vocale                           D.  none of the above

Questions 18-21.

DIRECTIONS:  Questions 18 through 21 are to be answered on the basis of the following list of
employees.

        Robertson, Aaron
        Bacon, Gina
        Jerimiah, Trace
        Gillette, Stanley
        Jacks, Sharon

18.  Which employee name would come in third in alphabetized list?               18._____
     A.  Robertson, Aaron                 B.  Jerimiah, Trace
     C.  Gillette, Stanley                D.  Jacks, Sharon

19.  Which employee's first name starts with the letter in the alphabet that is       19._____
     five letters after the first letter of their last name?
     A.  Jerimiah, Trace                  B.  Bacon, Gina
     C.  Jacks, Sharon                    D.  Gillette, Stanley

20.  How many employees have last names that are exactly five letters long?       20._____
     A.  1                 B.  2                 C.  3                 D.  4

21. How many of the employees have either a first or last name that starts with the letter "G"?
    A. 1          B. 2          C. 4          D. 5

Questions 22-25.

DIRECTIONS:   Questions 22 through 25 are to be answered on the basis of the following chart.

| Bicycle Sales (Model #34JA32) | | | | | | | |
|---|---|---|---|---|---|---|---|
| Country | May | June | July | August | September | October | Total |
| Germany | 34 | 47 | 45 | 54 | 56 | 60 | 296 |
| Britain | 40 | 44 | 36 | 47 | 47 | 46 | 260 |
| Ireland | 37 | 32 | 32 | 32 | 34 | 33 | 200 |
| Portugal | 14 | 14 | 14 | 16 | 17 | 14 | 89 |
| Italy | 29 | 29 | 28 | 31 | 29 | 31 | 177 |
| Belgium | 22 | 24 | 24 | 26 | 25 | 23 | 144 |
| Total | 176 | 198 | 179 | 206 | 208 | 207 | 1166 |

22. What percentage of the overall total was sold to the German importer?
    A. 25.3%          B. 22%          C. 24.1%          D. 23%

22._____

23. What percentage of the overall total was sold in September?
    A. 24.1%          B. 25.6%          C. 17.9%          D. 24.6%

23._____

24. What is the average number of units per month imported into Belgium over the first four months shown?
    A. 26          B. 20          C. 24          D. 31

24._____

25. If you look at the three smallest importers, what is their total import percentage?
    A. 35.1%          B. 37.1%          C. 40%          D. 28%

25._____

# KEY (CORRECT ANSWERS)

| | | | | |
|---|---|---|---|---|
| 1. | A | | 11. | B |
| 2. | A | | 12. | C |
| 3. | D | | 13. | C |
| 4. | D | | 14. | B |
| 5. | C | | 15. | D |
| | | | | |
| 6. | D | | 16. | C |
| 7. | A | | 17. | D |
| 8. | B | | 18. | D |
| 9. | D | | 19. | B |
| 10. | C | | 20. | B |

| | |
|---|---|
| 21. | B |
| 22. | A |
| 23. | C |
| 24. | C |
| 25. | A |

# TEST 4

DIRECTIONS: Each question or incomplete statement is followed by several suggested answers or completions. Select the one that BEST answers the question or completes the statement. *PRINT THE LETTER OF THE CORRECT ANSWER IN THE SPACE AT THE RIGHT.*

Questions 1-6.

DIRECTIONS: In answering Questions 1 through 6, choose the sentence that represents the BEST example of English grammar.

1.   A.   Joey and me want to go on a vacation next week.                              1._____
     B.   Gary told Jim he would need to take some time off.
     C.   If turning six years old, Jim's uncle would teach Spanish to him.
     D.   Fax a copy of your resume to Ms. Perez and me.

2.   A.   Jerry stood in line for almost two hours.                                     2._____
     B.   The reaction to my engagement was less exciting than I thought it would be.
     C.   Carlos and me have done great work on this project.
     D.   Two parts of the speech needs to be revised before tomorrow.

3.   A.   Arriving home, the alarm was tripped.                                         3._____
     B.   Jonny is regarded as a stand up guy, a responsible parent, and he doesn't give up until a task is finished.
     C.   Each employee must submit a drug test each month.
     D.   One of the documents was incinerated in the explosion.

4.   A.   As soon as my parents get home, I told them I finished all of my chores.      4._____
     B.   I asked my teacher to send me my missing work, check my absences, and how did I do on my test.
     C.   Matt attempted to keep it concealed from Jenny and me.
     D.   If Mary or him cannot get work done on time, I will have to split them up.

5.   A.   Driving to work, the traffic report warned him of an accident on Highway 47.  5._____
     B.   Jimmy has performed well this season.
     C.   Since finishing her degree, several job offers have been given to Cam.
     D.   Our boss is creating unstable conditions for we employees.

6.   A.   The thief was described as a tall man with a wiry mustache weighing approximately 150 pounds.   6._____
     B.   She gave Patrick and I some more time to finish our work.
     C.   One of the books that he ordered was damaged in shipping.
     D.   While talking on the rotary phone, the car Jim was driving skidded off the road.

Questions 7-9.

DIRECTIONS:   Questions 7 through 9 are to be answered on the basis of the following graph.

| Ice Lake Frozen Flight (2002-2013) | | |
|---|---|---|
| Year | Number of Participants | Temperature (Fahrenheit) |
| 2002 | 22 | 4° |
| 2003 | 50 | 33° |
| 2004 | 69 | 18° |
| 2005 | 104 | 22° |
| 2006 | 108 | 24° |
| 2007 | 288 | 33° |
| 2008 | 173 | 9° |
| 2009 | 598 | 39° |
| 2010 | 698 | 26° |
| 2011 | 696 | 30° |
| 2012 | 777 | 28° |
| 2013 | 578 | 32° |

7.   Which two year span had the LARGEST difference between temperatures?               7.____
     A.  2002 and 2003              B.  2011 and 2012
     C.  2008 and 2009              D.  2003 and 2004

8.   How many total people participated in the years after the temperature               8.____
     reached at least 29°?
     A.  2,295            B.  1,717            C.  2,210            D.  4,543

9.   In 2007, the event saw 288 participants, while in 2008 that number               9.____
     dropped to 173.  Which of the following reasons BEST explains the drop in
     participants?
     A.  The event had not been going on that long and people didn't know about
         it.
     B.  The lake water wasn't cold enough to have people jump in.
     C.  The temperature was too cold for many people who would have normally
         participated.
     D.  None of the above reasons explain the drop in participants.

10.  In the following list of numbers, how many times does 4 come just after 2               10.____
     when 2 comes just after an odd number?
     23652476538986324885724863924 24
     A.  2            B.  3            C.  4            D.  5

11.  Which choice below lists the letter that is as far after B as S is after N in               11.____
     the alphabet?
     A.  G            B.  H            C.  I            D.  J

Questions 12-15.

DIRECTIONS: Questions 12 through 15 are to be answered on the basis of the following directory and list of changes.

| Directory | | |
|---|---|---|
| Name | Emp. Type | Position |
| Julie Taylor | Warehouse | Packer |
| James King | Office | Administrative Assistant |
| John Williams | Office | Salesperson |
| Ray Moore | Warehouse | Maintenance |
| Kathleen Byrne | Warehouse | Supervisor |
| Amy Jones | Office | Salesperson |
| Paul Jonas | Office | Salesperson |
| Lisa Wong | Warehouse | Loader |
| Eugene Lee | Office | Accountant |
| Bruce Lavine | Office | Manager |
| Adam Gates | Warehouse | Packer |
| Will Suter | Warehouse | Packer |
| Gary Lorper | Office | Accountant |
| Jon Adams | Office | Salesperson |
| Susannah Harper | Office | Salesperson |

Directory Updates:
- Employee e-mail address will adhere to the following guidelines: lastnamefirstname@apexindustries.com (ex. Susannah Harper is harpersusannah@apexindustries.com). Currently, employees in the warehouse share one e-mail, distribution@apexindustries.com.
- The "Loader" position was now be referred to as "Specialist I"
- Adam Gates has accepted a Supervisor position within the Warehouse and is no longer a Packer. All warehouses employees report to the two Supervisors and all office employees report to the Manager.

12. Amy Jones tried to send an e-mail to Adam Gates, but it wouldn't send. Which of the following offers the BEST explanation?
    A. Amy put Adam's first name first and then his last name.
    B. Adam doesn't check his e-mail, so he wouldn't know if he received the e-mail or not.
    C. Adam does not have his own e-mail.
    D. Office employees are not allowed to send e-mails to each other.

12.____

13. How many Packers currently work for Apex Industries?
    A. 2        B. 3        C. 4        D. 5

13.____

14. What position does Lisa Wong currently hold?
    A. Specialist I              B. Secretary
    C. Administrative Assistant  D. Loader

14.____

15. If an employee wanted to contact the office manager, which of the        15.____
following e-mails should the e-mail be sent to?
    A. officemanager@apexindustries.com
    B. brucelavine@apexindustries.com
    C. lavinebruce@apexindustries.com
    D. distribution@apexindustries.com

Questions 16-19.

DIRECTIONS:   In answering Questions 16 through 19, compare the three names, numbers or
              addresses.

16. Smiley Yarnell        Smiley Yarnel         Smily Yarnell       16.____
    A. All three are exactly alike.
    B. The first and second are exactly alike.
    C. The second and third are exactly alike.
    D. All three are different.

17. 1583 Theater Drive    1583 Theater Drive    1583 Theatre Drive    17.____
    A. All three are exactly alike.
    B. The first and second are exactly alike.
    C. The second and third are exactly alike.
    D. All three are different.

18. 3341893212        3341893212        3341893212      18.____
    A. All three are exactly alike.
    B. The first and second are exactly alike.
    C. The second and third are exactly alike.
    D. All three are different.

19. Douglass Watkins    Douglas Watkins    Douglass Watkins    19.____
    A. All three are exactly alike.
    B. The first and second are exactly alike.
    C. The second and third are exactly alike.
    D. All three are different.

Questions 20-24.

DIRECTIONS:   In answering Questions 20 through 24, you will be presented with a word.
              Choose the synonym that BEST represents the word in question.

20. Flexible                                        20.____
    A. delicate     B. inflammable  C. strong    D. pliable

21. Alternative                                  21.____
    A. choice      B. moderate   C. lazy     D. value

22. Corroborate                22.____
  A. examine  B. explain  C. verify  D. explain

23. Respiration                23.____
  A. recovery  B. breathing  C. sweating  D. selfish

24. Negligent                24.____
  A. lazy  B. moderate  C. hopeless  D. lax

25. Plumber is to Wrench as Painter is to      25.____
  A. pipe  B. shop  C. hammer  D. brush

# KEY (CORRECT ANSWERS)

| 1. | D | | 11. | A |
|----|---|---|-----|---|
| 2. | A | | 12. | C |
| 3. | D | | 13. | A |
| 4. | C | | 14. | A |
| 5. | B | | 15. | C |
| 6. | C | | 16. | D |
| 7. | C | | 17. | B |
| 8. | B | | 18. | A |
| 9. | C | | 19. | B |
| 10. | C | | 20. | D |

| 21. | A |
|----|---|
| 22. | C |
| 23. | B |
| 24. | D |
| 25. | D |

# PREPARING WRITTEN MATERIAL

## PARAGRAPH REARRANGEMENT
## COMMENTARY

The sentences which follow are in scrambled order. You are to rearrange them in proper order and indicate the letter choice containing the correct answer at the space at the right.

Each group of sentences in this section is actually a paragraph presented in scrambled order. Each sentence in the group has a place in that paragraph; no sentence is to be left out. You are to read each group of sentences and decide upon the best order in which to put the sentences so as to form as well-organized paragraph.

The questions in this section measure the ability to solve a problem when all the facts relevant to its solution are not given.

More specifically, certain positions of responsibility and authority require the employee to discover connections between events sometimes, apparently, unrelated. In order to do this, the employee will find it necessary to correctly infer that unspecified events have probably occurred or are likely to occur. This ability becomes especially important when action must be taken on incomplete information.

Accordingly, these questions require competitors to choose among several suggested alternatives, each of which presents a different sequential arrangement of the events. Competitors must choose the MOST logical of the suggested sequences.

In order to do so, they may be required to draw on general knowledge to infer missing concepts or events that are essential to sequencing the given events. Competitors should be careful to infer only what is essential to the sequence. The plausibility of the wrong alternatives will always require the inclusion of unlikely events or of additional chains of events which are NOT essential to sequencing the given events.

It's very important to remember that you are looking for the best of the four possible choices, and that the best choice of all may not even be one of the answers you're given to choose from.

There is no one right way to these problems. Many people have found it helpful to first write out the order of the sentences, as they would have arranged them, on their scrap paper before looking at the possible answers. If their optimum answer is there, this can save them some time. If it isn't, this method can still give insight into solving the problem. Others find it most helpful to just go through each of the possible choices, contrasting each as they go along. You should use whatever method feels comfortable, and works, for you.

While most of these types of questions are not that difficult, we've added a higher percentage of the difficult type, just to give you more practice. Usually there are only one or two questions on this section that contain such subtle distinctions that you're unable to answer confidently, and you then may find yourself stuck deciding between two possible choices, neither of which you're sure about.

———

# Preparing Written Material

# EXAMINATION SECTION
## TEST 1

DIRECTIONS: The following groups of sentences need to be arranged in an order that makes sense. Select the letter preceding the sequence that represents the best sentence order. *PRINT THE LETTER OF THE CORRECT ANSWER IN THE SPACE AT THE RIGHT.*

Question 1                                                                                                        1.____

1.  The ostrich egg shell's legendary toughness makes it an excellent substitute for certain types of dishes or dinnerware, and in parts of Africa ostrich shells are cut and decorated for use as containers for water.
2.  Since prehistoric times, people have used the enormous egg of the ostrich as a part of their diet, a practice which has required much patience and hard work-to hard-boil an ostrich egg takes about four hours.
3.  Opening the egg's shell, which is rock hard and nearly an inch thick, requires heavy tools, such as a saw or chisel; from inside, a baby ostrich must use a hornlike projection on its beak as a miniature pick-axe to escape from the egg.
4.  The offspring of all higher-order animals originate from single egg cells that are carried by mothers, and most of these eggs are relatively small, often microscopic.
5.  The egg of the African ostrich, however, weighs a massive thirty pounds, making it the largest single cell on earth, and a common object of human curiosity and wonder.

The best order is

A.  5 4 1 2 3
B.  1 4 5 3 2
C.  4 2 3 5 1
D.  4 5 2 3 1

Question 2                                                                                                        2.____

1.  Typically only a few feet high on the open sea, individual tsunami have been known to circle the entire globe two or three times if their progress is not interrupted, but are not usually dangerous until they approach the shallow water that surrounds land masses.
2.  Some of the most terrifying and damaging hazards caused by earthquakes are tsunami, which were once called "tidal waves"— a poorly chosen name, since these waves have nothing to do with tides.
3.  Then a wave, slowed by the sudden drag on the lower part of its moving water column, will pile upon itself, sometimes reaching a height of over 100 feet.
4.  Tsunami (Japanese for "great harbor wave") are seismic waves that are caused by earthquakes near oceanic trenches, and once triggered, can travel up to 600 miles an hour on the open ocean.
5.  A land-shoaling tsunami is capable of extraordinary destruction; some tsunami have deposited large boats miles inland, washed out two-foot-thick seawalls, and scattered locomotive trains over long distances.

The best order is

A.  4 1 3 2 5
B.  1 3 4 2 5
C.  5 1 3 2 4
D.  2 4 1 3 5

Question 3                                                                                          3._____

1. Soon, by the 1940's, jazz was the most popular type of music among American intellectu-
   als and college students.
2. In the early days of jazz, it was considered "lowdown" music, or music that was played only
   in rough, disreputable bars and taverns.
3. However, jazz didn't take long to develop from early ragtime melodies into more complex,
   sophisticated forms, such as Charlie Parker's "bebop" style of jazz.
4. After charismatic band leaders such as Duke Ellington and Count Basic brought jazz to a
   larger audience, and jazz continued to evolve into more complicated forms, white audi-
   ences began to accept and even to enjoy the new American art form.
5. Many white Americans, who then dictated the tastes of society, were wary of music that
   was played almost exclusively in black clubs in the poorer sections of cities and towns.

   The best order is

   A.  5 4 3 2 1
   B.  2 5 3 4 1
   C.  4 5 3 1 2
   D.  1 2 4 3 5

Question 4                                                                                          4._____

1. Then, hanging in a windless place, the magnetized end of the needle would always point to
   the south.
2. The needle could then be balanced on the rim of a cup, or the edge of a fingernail, but this
   balancing act was hard to maintain, and the needle often fell off.
3. Other needles would point to the north, and it was important for any traveler finding his way
   with a compass to remember which kind of magnetized needle he was carrying.
4. To make some of the earliest compasses in recorded history, ancient Chinese "magicians"
   would rub a needle with a piece of magnetized iron called a lodestone.
5. A more effective method of keeping the needle free to swing with its magnetic pull was to
   attach a strand of silk to the center of the needle with a tiny piece of wax.

   The best order is

   A.  4 2 5 1 3
   B.  4 3 5 2 1
   C.  4 5 2 1 3
   D.  4 1 3 5 2

Question 5                                                                5._____

1. The now-famous first mate of the *HMS Bounty,* Fletcher Christian, founded one of the world's most peculiar civilizations in 1790.
2. The men knew they had just committed a crime for which they could be hanged, so they set sail for Pitcairn, a remote, abandoned island in the far eastern region of the Polynesian archipelago, accompanied by twelve Polynesian women and six men.
3. In a mutiny that has become legendary, Christian and the others forced Captain Bligh into a lifeboat and set him adrift off the coast of Tonga in April of 1789.
4. In early 1790, the *Bounty* landed at Pitcairn Island, where the men lived out the rest of their lives and founded an isolated community which to this day includes direct descendants of Christian and the other crewmen.
5. The *Bounty,* commanded by Captain William Bligh, was in the middle of a global voyage, and Christian and his shipmates had come to the conclusion that Bligh was a reckless madman who would lead them to their deaths unless they took the ship from him.

The best order is

    A.  4 5 3 2 1
    B.  1 3 5 2 4
    C.  1 5 3 2 4
    D.  3 1 5 4 2

Question 6                                                                6._____

1. But once the vines had been led to make orchids, the flowers had to be carefully hand-pollinated, because unpollinated orchids usually lasted less than a day, wilting and dropping off the vine before it had even become dark.
2. The Totonac farmers discovered that looping a vine back around once it reached a five-foot height on its host tree would cause the vine to flower.
3. Though they knew how to process the fruit pods and extract vanilla's flavoring agent, the Totonacs also knew that a wild vanilla vine did not produce abundant flowers or fruit.
4. Wild vines climbed along the trunks and canopies of trees, and this constant upward growth diverted most of the vine's energy to making leaves instead of the orchid flowers that, once pollinated, would produce the flavorful pods.
5. Hundreds of years before vanilla became a prized food flavoring in Europe and the Western World, the Totonac Indians of the Mexican Gulf Coast were skilled cultivators of the vanilla vine, whose fruit they literally worshipped as a goddess.

The best order is

    A.  2 3 4 1 5
    B.  2 4 3 1 5
    C.  5 3 4 2 1
    D.  3 4 1 2 5

## Question 7
7.____

1. Once airborne, the spider is at the mercy of the air currents—usually the spider takes a brief journey, traveling close to the ground, but some have been found in air samples collected as high as 10,000 feet, or been reported landing on ships far out at sea.
2. Once a young spider has hatched, it must leave the environment into which it was born as quickly as possible, in order to avoid competing with its hundreds of brothers and sisters for food.
3. The silk rises into warm air currents, and as soon as the pull feels adequate the spider lets go and drifts up into the air, suspended from the silk strand in the same way that a person might parasail.
4. To help young spiders do this, many species have adapted a practice known as "aerial dispersal," or, in common speech, "ballooning."
5. A spider that wants to leave its surroundings quickly will climb to the top of a grass stem or twig, face into the wind, and aim its back end into the air, releasing a long stream of silk from the glands near the tip of its abdomen.

The best order is

A. 5 4 2 3 1
B. 5 2 4 1 3
C. 2 5 4 3 1
D. 2 4 5 3 1

## Question 8
8.____

1. For about a year, Tycho worked at a castle in Prague with a scientist named Johannes Kepler, but their association was cut short by another argument that drove Kepler out of the castle, to later develop, on his own, the theory of planetary orbits.
2. Tycho found life without a nose embarrassing, so he made a new nose for himself out of silver, which reportedly remained glued to his face for the rest of his life.
3. Tycho Brahe, the 17th-century Danish astronomer, is today more famous for his odd and arrogant personality than for any contribution he has made to our knowledge of the stars and planets.
4. Early in his career, as a student at Rostock University, Tycho got into an argument with the another student about who was the better mathematician, and the two became so angry that the argument turned into a sword fight, during which Tycho's nose was sliced off.
5. Later in his life, Tycho's arrogance may have kept him from playing a part in one of the greatest astronomical discoveries in history: the elliptical orbits of the solar system's planets.

The best order is

A. 1 4 2 3 5
B. 4 2 3 5 1
C. 4 2 1 3 5
D. 3 4 2 5 1

Question 9                                                                  9._____

1.  The processionaries are so used to this routine that if a person picks up the end of a silk line and brings it back to the origin—creating a closed circle—the caterpillars may travel around and around for days, sometimes starving ar freezing, without changing course.
2.  Rather than relying on sight or sound, the other caterpillars, who are lined up end-to-end behind the leader, travel to and from their nests by walking on this silk line, and each will reinforce it by laying down its own marking line as it passes over.
3.  In order to insure the safety of individuals, the processionary caterpillar nests in a tree with dozens of other caterpillars, and at night, when it is safest, they all leave together in search of food.
4.  The processionary caterpillar of the European continent is a perfect illustration of how much some insect species rely on instinct in their daily routines.
5.  As they leave their nests, the processionaries form a single-file line behind a leader who spins and lays out a silk line to mark the chosen path.

The best order is

A.  4 3 5 2 1
B.  3 5 4 2 1
C.  3 5 2 1 4
D.  4 5 3 1 2

Question 10                                                                 10._____

1.  Often, the child is also given a handcrafted walker or push cart, to provide support for its first upright explorations.
2.  In traditional Indian families, a child's first steps are celebrated as a ceremonial event, rooted in ancient myth.
3.  These carts are often intricately designed to resemble the chariot of Krishna, an important figure in Indian mythology.
4.  The sound of these anklet bells is intended to mimic the footsteps of the legendary child Rama, who is celebrated in devotional songs throughout India.
5.  When the child's parents see that the child is ready to begin walking, they will fit it with specially designed ankle bracelets, adorned with gently ringing bells.

The best order is

A.  2 3 4 1 5
B.  2 5 3 1 4
C.  5 4 1 3 2
D.  5 3 2 1 4

Question 11

1. The settlers planted Osage orange all across Middle America, and today long lines and rectangles of Osage orange trees can still be seen on the prairies, running along the former boundaries of farms that no longer exist.
2. After trying sod walls and water-filled ditches with no success, American farmers began to look for a plant that was adaptable to prairie weather, and that could be trimmed into a hedge that was "pig-tight, horse-high, and bull-strong."
3. The tree, so named because it bore a large (but inedible) fruit the size of an orange, was among the sturdiest and hardiest of American trees, and was prized among Native Americans for the strength and flexibility of bows which were made from its wood.
4. The first people to practice agriculture on the American flatlands were faced with an important problem: what would they use to fence their land in a place that was almost entirely without trees or rocks?
5. Finally, an Illinois farmer brought the settlers a tree that was native to the land between the Red and Arkansas rivers, a tree called the Osage orange.

The best order is

A. 2 1 5 3 4
B. 1 2 3 4 5
C. 4 2 5 3 1
D. 4 2 1 3 5

Question 12

1. After about ten minutes of such spirited and complicated activity, the head dancer is free to make up his or her own movements while maintaining the interest of the New Year's crowd.
2. The dancer will then perform a series of leg kicks, while at the same time operating the lion's mouth with his own hand and moving the ears and eyes by means of a string which is attached to the dancer's own mouth.
3. The most difficult role of this dance belongs to the one who controls the lion's head; this person must lead all the other "parts" of the lion through the choreographed segments of the dance.
4. The head dancer begins with a complex series of steps, alternately stepping forward with the head raised, and then retreating a few steps while lowering the head, a movement that is intended to create the impression that the lion is keeping a watchful eye for anything evil.
5. When performing a traditional Chinese New Year's lion dance, several performers must fit themselves inside a large lion costume and work together to enact different parts of the dance.

The best order is

A. 5 3 4 2 1
B. 3 4 2 5 1
C. 3 1 5 4 2
D. 4 2 3 5 1

Question 13

13.____

1. For many years the shell of the chambered nautilus was treasured in Europe for its beauty and intricacy, but collectors were unaware that they were in possession of the structure that marked a "missing link" in the evolution of marine mollusks.
2. The nautilus, however, evolved a series of enclosed chambers in its shell, and invented a new use for the structure: the shell began to serve as a buoyancy device.
3. Equipped with this new flotation device, the nautilus did not need the single, muscular foot of its predecessors, but instead developed flaps, tentacles, and a gentle form of jet propulsion that transformed it into the first mollusk able to take command of its own destiny and explore a three-dimensional world.
4. By pumping and adjusting air pressure into the chambers, the nautilus could spend the day resting on the bottom, and then rise toward the surface at night in search of food.
5. The nautilus shell looks like a large snail shell, similar to those of its ancestors, who used their shells as protective coverings while they were anchored to the sea floor.

The best order is

A. 5 2 4 1 3
B. 5 1 2 3 4
C. 1 2 5 3 4
D. 1 5 2 4 3

Question 14

14.____

1. While France and England battled for control of the region, the Acadiens prospered on the fertile farmland, which was finally secured by England in 1713.
2. Early in the 17<sup>th</sup> century, settlers from western France founded a colony called Acadie in what is now the Canadian province of Nova Scotia.
3. At this time, English officials feared the presence of spies among the Acadiens who might be loyal to their French homeland, and the Acadiens were deported to spots along the Atlantic and Caribbean shores of America.
4. The French settlers remained on this land, under English rule, for around forty years, until the beginning of the French and Indian War, another conflict between France and England.
5. As the Acadien refugees drifted toward a final home in southern Louisiana, neighbors shortened their name to "Cadien," and finally "Cajun," the name which the descendants of early Acadiens still call themselves.

The best order is

A. 1 4 2 3 5
B. 2 1 3 5 4
C. 2 1 4 3 5
D. 5 2 3 4 1

Question 15                                                                                                     15.\_\_\_\_\_

1.  Traditional households in the Eastern and Western regions of Africa serve two meals a day-one at around noon, and the other in the evening.
2.  The starch is then used in the way that Americans might use a spoon, to scoop up a portion of the main dish on the person's plate.
3.  The reason for the starch's inclusion in every meal has to do with taste as well as nutrition; African food can be very spicy, and the starch is known to cool the burning effect of the main dish.
4.  When serving these meals, the main dish is usually served on individual plates, and the starch is served on a communal plate, from which diners break off a piece of bread or scoop rice or fufu in their fingers.
5.  The typical meals usually consist of a thick stew or soup as the main course, and an accompanying starch—either bread, rice, *or fufu, a* starchy grain paste similar in consistency to mashed potatoes.

The best order is

A.  5 2 3 4 1
B.  5 1 4 3 2
C.  1 4 5 3 2
D.  1 5 4 2 3

Question 16                                                                                                     16.\_\_\_\_\_

1.  In the early days of the American Midwest, Indiana settlers sometimes came together to hold an event called an apple peeling, where neighboring settlers gathered at the home-stead of a host family to help prepare the hosts' apple crop for cooking, canning, and mak-ing apple butter.
2.  At the beginning of the event, each peeler sat down in front of a ten- or twenty-gallon stone jar and was given a crock of apples and a paring knife.
3.  Once a peeler had finished with a crock, another was placed next to him; if the peeler was an unmarried man, he kept a strict count of the number of apples he had peeled, because the winner was allowed to kiss the girl of his choice.
4.  The peeling usually ended by 9:30 in the evening, when the neighbors gathered in the host family's parlor for a dance social.
5.  The apples were peeled, cored, and quartered, and then placed into the jar.

The best order is

A.  1 5 3 4 2
B.  2 5 3 4 1
C.  1 2 5 3 4
D.  2 1 5 4 3

Question 17                                                                 17._____

  1.  If your pet turtle is a land turtle and is native to temperate climates, it will stop eating some time in October, which should be your cue to prepare the turtle for hibernation.

  2.  The box should then be covered with a wire screen, which will protect the turtle from any rodents or predators that might want to take advantage of a motionless and helpless animal.

  3.  When your turtle hasn't eaten for a while and appears ready to hibernate, it should be moved to its winter quarters, most likely a cellar or garage, where the temperature should range between $40^\circ$ and $45^\circ$ F.

  4.  Instead of feeding the turtle, you should bathe it every day in warm water, to encourage the turtle to empty its intestines in preparation for its long winter sleep.

  5.  Here the turtle should be placed in a well-ventilated box whose bottom is covered with a moisture-absorbing layer of clay beads, and then filled three-fourths full with almost dry peat moss or wood chips, into which the turtle will burrow and sleep for several months.

The best order is

    A.  1 4 3 5 2
    B.  3 4 2 5 1
    C.  3 2 4 1 5
    D.  4 5 2 3 1

Question 18                                                                 18._____

  1.  Once he has reached the nest, the hunter uses two sturdy bamboo poles like huge chopsticks to pull the nest away from the mountainside, into a large basket that will be lowered to people waiting below.

  2.  The world's largest honeybees colonize the Nepalese mountainsides, building honeycombs as large as a person on sheer rock faces that are often hundreds of feet high.

  3.  In the remote mountain country of Nepal, a small band of "honey hunters" carry out a tradition so ancient that 10,000 year-old drawings of the practice have been found in the caves of Nepal.

  4.  To harvest the honey and beeswax from these combs, a honey hunter climbs above the nests, lowers a long bamboo-fiber ladder over the cliff, and then climbs down.

  5.  Throughout this dangerous practice, the hunter is stung repeatedly, and only the veterans, with skin that has been toughened over the years, are able to return from a hunt without the painful swelling caused by stings.

The best order is

    A.  2 4 3 5 1
    B.  2 4 1 5 3
    C.  5 3 2 4 1
    D.  3 2 4 1 5

Question 19                                                                                          19.____

1. After the Romans left Britain, there were relentless attacks on the islands from the barbarian tribes of northern Germany–the Angles, Saxons, and Jutes.
2. As the empire weakened, Roman soldiers withdrew from Britain, leaving behind a country that continued to practice the Christian religion that had been introduced by the Romans.
3. Early Latin writings tell of a Christian warrior named Arturius (Arthur, in English) who led the British citizens to defeat these barbarian invaders, and brought an extended period of peace to the lands of Britain.
4. Long ago, the British Isles were part of the far-flung Roman Empire that extended across most of Europe and into Africa and Asia.
5. The romantic legend of King Arthur and his knights of the Round Table, one of the most popular and widespread stories of all time, appears to have some foundation in history.

The best order is

A.  5 4 3 2 1
B.  5 4 2 1 3
C.  4 5 2 3 1
D.  4 3 2 1 5

Question 20                                                                                          20.____

1. The cylinder was allowed to cool until it sould stand on its own, and then it was cut from the tube and split down the side with a single straight cut.
2. Nineteenth-century glassmakers, who had not yet discovered the glazier's modern techniques for making panes of glass, had to create a method for converting their blown glass into flat sheets.
3. The bubble was then pierced at the end to make a hole that opened up while the glassmaker gently spun it, creating a cylinder of glass.
4. Turned on its side and laid on a conveyor belt, the cylinder was strengthened, or tempered, by being heated again and cooled very slowly, eventually flattening out into a single rectangular piece of glass.
5. To do this, the glassmaker dipped the end of a long tube into melted glass and blew into the other end of the tube, creating an expanding bubble of glass.

The best order is

A.  2 5 3 4 1
B.  2 4 5 3 1
C.  3 5 2 4 1
D.  3 1 4 5 2

Question 21                                                                          21._____

1. The splints are almost always hidden, but horses are occasionally born whose splinted toes project from the leg on either side, just above the hoof.
2. The second and fourth toes remained, but shrank to thin splints of bone that fused invisibly to the horse's leg bone.
3. Horses are unique among mammals, having evolved feet that each end in what is essentially a single toe, capped by a large, sturdy hoof.
4. Julius Caesar, an emperor of ancient Rome, was said to have owned one of these three-toed horses, and considered it so special that he would not permit anyone else to ride it.
5. Though the horse's earlier ancestors possessed the traditional mammalian set of five toes on each foot, the horse has retained only its third toe; its first and fifth toes disappeared completely as the horse evolved.

The best order is

   A.  3 5 2 1 4
   B.  5 3 2 4 1
   C.  3 2 5 1 4
   D.  5 2 3 1 4

Question 22                                                                          22._____

1. The new building materials—some of which are twenty feet long, and weigh nearly six tons—were transported to Pohnpei on rafts, and were brought into their present position by using hibiscus fiber ropes and leverage to move the stone columns upward along the inclined trunks of coconut palm trees.
2. The ancestors built great fires to heat the stone, and then poured cool seawater on the columns, which caused the stone to contract and split along natural fracture lines.
3. The now-abandoned enclave of Nan Madol, a group of 92 man-made islands off the shore of the Micronesian island of Pohnpei, is estimated to have been built around the year 500 A.D.
4. The islanders say their ancestors quarried stone columns from a nearby island, where large basalt columns were formed by the cooling of molten lava.
5. The structures of Nan Madol are remarkable for the sheer size of some of the stone "logs" or columns that were used to create the walls of the offshore community, and today anthropologists can only rely on the information of existing local people for clues about how Nan Madol was built.

The best order is

   A.  5 4 3 2 1
   B.  5 3 1 4 2
   C.  3 5 4 2 1
   D.  3 1 4 2 5

## Question 23

1. One of the most easily manipulated substances on earth, glass can be made into ceramic tiles that are composed of over 90% air.
2. NASA's space shuttles are the first spacecraft ever designed to leave and re-enter the earth's atmosphere while remaining intact.
3. These ceramic tiles are such effective insulators that when a tile emerges from the oven in which it was fired, it can be held safely in a person's hand by the edges while its interior still glows at a temperature well over 2000° F.
4. Eventually, the engineers were led to a material that is as old as our most ancient civiliza-tionsglass.
5. Because the temperature during atmospheric re-entry is so incredibly hot, it took NASA's engineers some time to find a substance capable of protecting the shuttles.

The best order is

A. 5 2 1 3 4
B. 2 5 4 1 3
C. 2 3 1 2 5
D. 5 4 3 1 2

## Question 24

1. The secret to teaching any parakeet to talk is patience, and the understanding that when a bird "talks," it is simply imitating what it hears, rather than putting ideas into words.
2. You should stay just out of sight of the bird and repeat the phrase you want it to learn, for at least fifteen minutes every morning and evening.
3. It is important to leave the bird without any words of encouragement or farewell; otherwise it might combine stray remarks or phrases, such as "Good night," with the phrase you are trying to teach it.
4. For this reason, to train your bird to imitate your words you should keep it free of any dis-tractions, especially other noises, while you are giving it "lessons."
5. After your repetition, you should quietly leave the bird alone for a while, to think over what it has just heard.

The best order is

A. 1 4 2 5 3
B. 1 2 4 3 5
C. 3 2 1 5 4
D. 3 1 5 4 2

## Question 25

25._____

1. As a school approaches, fishermen from neighboring communities join their fishing boats together as a fleet, and string their gill nets together to make a huge fence that is held up by cork floats.
2. At a signal from the party leaders, or *nakura,* the family members pound the sides of the boats or beat the water with long poles, creating a sudden and deafening noise.
3. The fishermen work together to drag the trap into a half-circle that may reach 300 yards in diameter, and then the families move their boats to form the other half of the circle around the school of fish.
4. The school of fish flee from the commotion into the awaiting trap, where a final wall of net is thrown over the open end of the half-circle, securing the day's haul.
5. Indonesian people from the area around the Sulu islands live on the sea, in floating villages made of lashed-together or stilted homes, and make much of their living by fishing their home waters for migrating schools of snapper, scad, and other fish.

The best order is

A. 1 5 3 4 2
B. 1 2 4 3 5
C. 5 1 2 3 4
D. 5 1 3 2 4

---

# KEY (CORRECT ANSWERS)

| | | | |
|---|---|---|---|
| 1. D | | 11. C | |
| 2. D | | 12. A | |
| 3. B | | 13. D | |
| 4. A | | 14. C | |
| 5. C | | 15. D | |
| 6. C | | 16. C | |
| 7. D | | 17. A | |
| 8. D | | 18. D | |
| 9. A | | 19. B | |
| 10. B | | 20. A | |

21. A
22. C
23. B
24. A
25. D

---

# PREPARING WRITTEN MATERIAL

# EXAMINATION SECTION
## TEST 1

DIRECTIONS:    Each of Questions 1 through 5 consists of a sentence which may or may not be an example of good formal English usage.

Examine each sentence, considering grammar, punctuation, spelling, capitalization, and awkwardness. Then choose the correct statement about it from the four options below it.

If the English usage in the sentence given is better than any of the changes suggested in options B, C, or D, pick option A. (Do not pick an option that will change the meaning of the sentence.

1.   I don't know who could possibly of broken it.                                         1._____

    A.   This is an example of good formal English usage.
    B.   The word "who" should be replaced by the word "whom."
    C.   The word "of" should be replaced by the word "have."
    D.   The word "broken" should be replaced by the word "broke."

2.   Telephoning is easier than to write.                                         2._____

    A.   This is an example of good formal English usage.
    B.   The word "telephoning" should be spelled "telephoneing."
    C.   The word "than" should be replaced by the word "then."
    D.   The words "to write" should be replaced by the word "writing."

3.   The two operators who have been assigned to these consoles are on vacation.      3._____

    A.   This is an example of good formal English usage.
    B.   A comma should be placed after the word "operators."
    C.   The word "who" should be replaced by the word "whom."
    D.   The word "are" should be replaced by the word "is."

4.   You were suppose to teach me how to operate a plugboard.                       4._____

    A.   This is an example of good formal English usage.
    B.   The word "were" should be replaced by the word "was."
    C.   The word "suppose" should be replaced by the word "supposed."
    D.   The word "teach" should be replaced by the word "learn."

5.   If you had taken my advice; you would have spoken with him.                    5._____

    A.   This is an example of good formal English usage.
    B.   The word "advice" should be spelled "advise."
    C.   The words "had taken" should be replaced by the word "take."
    D.   The semicolon should be changed to a comma.

# KEY (CORRECT ANSWERS)

1. C
2. D
3. A
4. C
5. D

————

# TEST 2

DIRECTIONS:   Select the correct answer.

1. The *one* of the following sentences which is *MOST* acceptable from the viewpoint of cor-    1.____
   rect grammatical usage is:

   A.   I do not know which action will have worser results.
   B.   tie should of known better.
   C.   Both the officer on the scene, and his immediate supervisor, is charged with the
        responsibility.
   D.   An officer must have initiative because his supervisor will not always be available to
        answer questions.

2. The *one* of the following sentences which is *MOST* acceptable from the viewpoint of cor-    2.____
   rect grammatical usage is:

   A.   Of all the officers available, the better one for the job will be picked.
   B.   Strict orders were given to all the officers, except he.
   C.   Study of the law will enable you to perform your duties more efficiently.
   D.   It seems to me that you was wrong in failing to search the two men.

3. The *one* of the following sentences which does *NOT* contain a misspelled word is:    3.____

   A.   The duties you will perform are similiar to the duties of a patrolman.
   B.   Officers must be constantly alert to sieze the initiative.
   C.   Officers in this organization are not entitled to special privileges.
   D.   Any changes in procedure will be announced publically.

4. The *one* of the following sentences which does *NOT* contain a misspelled word is:    4.____

   A.   It will be to your advantage to keep your firearm in good working condition.
   B.   There are approximately fourty men on sick leave.
   C.   Your first duty will be to pursuade the person to obey the law.
   D.   Fires often begin in flameable material kept in lockers.

5. The *one* of the following sentences which does *NOT* contain a misspelled word is:    5.____

   A.   Officers are not required to perform technical maintainance.
   B.   He violated the regulations on two occasions.
   C.   Every employee will be held responable for errors.
   D.   This was his nineth absence in a year.

# KEY (CORRECT ANSWERS)

1. D
2. C
3. C
4. A
5. B

# TEST 3

DIRECTIONS: Select the correct answer.

1. You are answering a letter that was written on the letterhead of the ABC Company jind signed by James H. Wood, Treasurer. What is usually considered to be the correct salutation to use in your reply?

   A. Dear ABC Company:
   C. Dear Mr. Wood:
   B. Dear Sirs:
   D. Dear Mr. Treasurer:

1.____

2. Assume that one of your duties is to handle routine letters of inquiry from the public. The one of the following which is usually considered to be MOST desirable in replying to such a letter is a

   A. detailed answer handwritten on the original letter of inquiry
   B. phone call, since you can cover details more easily over the phone than in a letter
   C. short letter giving the specific information requested
   D. long letter discussing all possible aspects of the question raised

2.____

3. The CHIEF reason for dividing a letter into paragraphs is to

   A. make the message clear to the reader by starting a new paragraph for each new topic
   B. make a short letter occupy as much of the page as possible
   C. keep the reader's attention by providing a pause from time to time
   D. make the letter look neat and businesslike

3.____

4. Your superior has asked you to send an e-mail from your agency to a government agency in another city. He has written out the message and has indicated the name of the government agency.
   When you dictate the message to your secretary, which of the following items that your superior has NOT mentioned must you be sure to include?

   A. Today's date
   B. The full address of the government agency
   C. A polite opening such as "Dear Sirs"
   D. A final sentence such as "We would appreciate hearing from your agency in reply as soon as is convenient for you"

4.____

5. The one of the following sentence which is grammatically preferable to the others is:

   A. Our engineers will go over your blueprints so that you may have no problems in construction.
   B. For a long time he had been arguing that we, not he, are to blame for the confusion.
   C. I worked on this automobile for two hours and still cannot find out what is wrong with it.
   D. Accustomed to all kinds of hardships, fatigue seldom bothers veteran policemen.

5.____

# KEY (CORRECT ANSWERS)

1. C
2. C
3. A
4. B
5. A

————

# TEST 4

DIRECTIONS:  Select the correct answer.

1. Suppose that an applicant for a job as snow laborer presents a letter from a former
   employer stating: "John Smith has a pleasing manner and never got into an argument
   with his fellow employees. He was never late or absent." This letter

   A. indicates that with some training Smith will make a good snow gang boss
   B. presents no definite evidence of Smith's ability to do snow work
   C. proves definitely that Smith has never done any snow work before
   D. proves definitely that Smith will do better than average work as a snow laborer

   1.____

2. Suppose you must write a letter to a local organization in your section refusing a request
   in connection with collection of their refuse.
   You should *start* the letter by

   A. explaining in detail the consideration you gave the request
   B. praising the organization for its service to the community
   C. quoting the regulation which forbids granting the request
   D. stating your regret that the request cannot be granted

   2.____

3. Suppose a citizen writes in for information as to whether or not he may sweep refuse into
   the gutter. A Sanitation officer answers as follows:
   Dear Sir:
      No person is permitted to litter, sweep, throw or cast, or direct, suffer or permit any
   person under his control to litter, sweep, throw or cast any ashes, garbage, paper,
   dust, or other rubbish or refuse into any public street or place, vacant lot, air shaft,
   areaway, backyard or court.

   Very truly yours,<br>John Doe

   This letter is *poorly* written CHIEFLY because

   A. the opening is not indented
   B. the thought is not clear
   C. the tone is too formal and cold
   D. there are too many commas used

   3.____

4. A section of a disciplinary report written by a Sanitation officer states: "It is requested
   that subject Sanitation man be advised that his future activities be directed towards
   reducing his recurrent tardiness else disciplinary action will be initiated which may result
   in summary discharge." This section of the report is *poorly* written MAINLY because

   A. at least one word is misspelled
   B. it is not simply expressed
   C. more than one idea is expressed
   D. the purpose is not stated

   4.____

5. A section of a disciplinary report written by an officer states: "He comes in late. He takes    5.____
   too much time for lunch. He is lazy. I recommend his services be dispensed with."
   This section of the report is *poorly* written *MAINLY* because

    A. it ends with a preposition
    B. it is not well organized
    C. no supporting facts are stated
    D. the sentences are too simple

———————

# KEY (CORRECT ANSWERS)

    1. B
    2. D
    3. C
    4. B
    5. C

———————

# FOOD SERVICE GLOSSARY

## TABLE OF CONTENTS

# FOOD SERVICE GLOSSARY

## A

**ABSORPTION CAPABILITY**
 The property of flour to absorb and hold liquid.

**ACIDITY**
 Sourness or tartness in a food product; in yeast doughs, a condition indicating excess fermentation; a factor in generating carbon dioxide for cake leavening.

**AERATION**
 See LEAVENING.

**AEROBIC BACTERIA**
 Those that require the presence of free oxygen as found in the air for growth.

**A LA CARTE**
 On the menu alone, not in combination with a total meal.

**A LA KING**
 A dish served with a cream sauce, usually containing green peppers and pimentos, and sometimes mushrooms and onions.

**A LA MODE**
 In a fashion or the style of; for example, desserts served with ice cream or pot roast of beef cooked with vegetables.

**ALBUMEN**
 Egg white.

**AMBROSIA**
 A favorite southern dessert made of oranges, bananas, pineapple, and shredded coconut.

**AMEBA**
 A simple animal-like organism that grows in water.

**ANAEROBIC BACTERIA**
 Those that grow in oxygen-free atmosphere, deriving oxygen from solid or liquid materials and producing toxic substances.

**ANTIBIOTICS**
 Substances produced by microorganisms and capable of inhibiting or killing other microorganisms.

**ANTIOXIDANT**
 A chemical solution in which fruits and vegetables are dipped to prevent darkening.

ANTIPASTI or ANTIPASTO
An appetizer, or a spicy first course, consisting of relishes, cold sliced meats rolled with or without stuffings, fish, or other hors d'oeuvres eaten with a fork.

ANTISEPTIC
An agent that may or may not kill microorganisms, but does inhibit their growth. Peroxide is an example.

APPETIZER
A small portion of food or drink before or as the first course of a meal. These include a wide assortment of items ranging from cocktails, canapes, and hors d'oeuvres to plain fruit juices. The function of an appetizer is to pep up the appetite.

AU GRATIN
A thin surface crust formed by either bread or cheese, or both. Sometimes used with a cream sauce.

AU JUS
With natural juice. Roast rib au jus, for example, is beef served with unthickened gravy.

*B*

BACILLI
Cylindrical or rod-shaped bacteria responsible for such diseases as botulism, typhoid fever, and tuberculosis.

BACTERIA
Microscopic, one-cell microbes found in soil, water, and most material throughout nature. Some are responsible for disease and food spoilage, others are useful in industrial fermentation.

BACTERICIDE
Any substance that kills bacteria and related forms of life.

BAKE
To cook by dry heat in an oven. When applied to meats, it is called roasting.

BARBECUE
To roast or broil in a highly seasoned sauce.

BASTE
To moisten foods while cooking, especially while roasting meat. Melted fat, meat drippings, stock, water, or water and fat may be used.

BATTER
A homogeneous mixture of ingredients with liquid to make a mass that is of a soft plastic character.

BAVARIAN
A style of cooking that originated in the Bavarian section of Germany.

**BEAT**
    To make a mixture smooth or to introduce air by using a lifting motion with spoon or whip.

**BENCH TOLERANCE**
    The property of dough to ferment at a rate slow enough to prevent overfermentation while dough is being made up into units on the bench.

**BLANCH**
    To rinse with boiling water, drain, and rinse in cold water. Used for rice, macaroni, and other pastas to prevent sticking. For potatoes, to cook in hot, deep fat for a short time until clear but not brown.

**BLAND**
    Mild flavored, not stimulating to the taste.

**BLEACHED FLOUR**
    Flour that has been treated by a chemical to remove its natural color and make it white.

**BLEEDING**
    Dough that has been cut and left unsealed at the cut, thus permitting the escape of leavening gas. This term also applies to icing that bleeds.

**BLEND**
    To mix thoroughly two or more ingredients.

**BOIL**
    To cook in a liquid that bubbles actively during the time of cooking. The boiling temperature of water at sea level is 212° F.

**BOTULISM**
    Acute food poisoning caused by botulin (toxin) in food.

**BOUILLON**
    A clear soup made from beef or chicken stock or soup and gravy base.

**BRAISE**
    To brown meat or vegetables in a small amount of fat, then to cook slowly, covered, at simmering temperature in a small amount of liquid. The liquid may be juices rendered from meat, or added water, milk, or meat stock.

**BREAD**
    To coat with crumbs of bread or other food; or to dredge in seasoned flour, dip in a mixture of milk and slightly beaten eggs, and then dredge again in crumbs.

**BROIL**
    To cook under or over direct heat.

**BROWN**
    To cook, usually at medium or high heat, until the item of food darkens.

**BRUNSWICK STEW**
A main dish composed of a combination of poultry, meats, and vegetables.

**BUTTERFLY**
A method of cutting double chops (usually pork) from boneless loin strips. One side of each double chop is hinged together with a thin layer of meat.

**BUTTERHORNS**
Basic sweet dough cut and shaped like horns.

## C

**CACCIATORE**
Chicken cooked "hunter" style. Browned chicken is braised in a sauce made with tomatoes, other vegetables, stock, and herbs.

**CANAPE**
Any of many varieties of appetizers, usually spread on bread, toast, or crackers and eaten with the fingers.

**CANDY**
To cook in sugar or syrup.

**CARAMELIZED SUGAR**
Dry sugar heated with constant stirring until melted and dark in color, used for flavoring and coloring.

**CARBOHYDRATES**
Sugars and starches derived chiefly from fruits and vegetable sources and containing set amounts of carbon, hydrogen, and oxygen.

**CARBON DIOXIDE**
A colorless, tasteless edible gas obtained during fermentation or from a combination of soda and acid.

**CARRIERS**
Persons who harbor and disseminate germs without having symptoms of a disease. The individual has either had the disease at one time and temporarily continues to excrete the organism, or has never manifested symptoms because of good resistance to the disease.

**CHIFFONADE DRESSING**
A salad dressing containing chopped hard-cooked eggs and beets.

**CHIFFON CAKE**
A sponge cake containing liquid shortening.

**CHILI**
A special pepper or its fruits. Dried, ground chili peppers are used in chili powder.

**CHILI CON CARNE**
Ground beef and beans seasoned with chili powder.

**CHILL**
To place in a refrigerator or cool place until cold.

**CHOP**
To cut into pieces with a knife or chopper.

**CHOP SUEY**
A thick Chinese stew of thin slices of pork and various vegetables, such as bean sprouts, celery, and onions.

**CLEAR FLOUR**
Lower grade and higher ash content flour remaining after the patent flour has been separated. (Used in rye bread. )

**COAGULATE**
To thicken or form into a consistent mass.

**COAT**
To cover the entire surface of food with a selected mixture.

**CONDIMENTS**
Seasonings that in themselves furnish little nourishment, but which improve the flavor of food.

**CONGEALING POINT**
Temperature or time at which a liquid changes to a firm or plastic condition.

**COOKING LOSSES**
Loss of weight, liquid, or nutrients, and possibly a lowered palatability of a cooked food.

**COOL**
To let stand, usually at room temperature, until no longer warm to touch.

**CREAM**
To mix until smooth, sugar, shortening, and other ingredients; to incorporate air so that resultant mixture increases appreciably in volume and is thoroughly blended.

**CREAM PUFFS**
Baked puffs of cream-puff dough, which are hollow; usually filled with cream pudding, whipped topping, or ice cream.

**CREOLE**
A cooked sauce for poultry or shrimp. Usually served with rice.

**CRISP**
To make somewhat firm and brittle.

**CROUTONS**
Bread cut into small cubes and either fried or browned in the oven, according to the intended use. Used as a garnish, croutons are fried; as soup accompaniments, baked.

**CRULLERS**
Long, twisted doughnuts.

**CRUMB**
The soft part of bread or cake; a fragment of bread (see also BREAD).

**CRUST**
Hardened exterior of bread; pastry portion of pie.

**CRUSTING**
Formation of dry crust on the surface of doughs.

**CUBE**
To cut into approximately 1/4 to 1/2 inch squares.

**CURDLE**
To change into curd; to coagulate or thicken.

**CURING**
A form of processing meat, which improves its flavor and texture.

**CURRY**
A powder made from many spice ingredients and used as a seasoning for Indian and Oriental-type dishes, such as shrimp and chicken curry.

**CUSTOM FOODS (RATION-DENSE)**
Various types of labor- and space-saving foods, including canned, concentrated, dehydrated, frozen, and prefabricated items.

**CUT IN (as for shortening)**
To combine firm shortening and flour with pastry blender or knife.

## D

**DANISH PASTRY**
A flaky yeast dough having butter or shortening rolled into it.

**DASH**
A scant 1/8 teaspoon.

**DEVILED**
A highly seasoned, chopped, ground, or whole mixture served hot or cold.

**DICE**
To cut into 1/4 inch or smaller cubes.

**DISINFECTANT**
A chemical agent that destroys bacteria and other harmful organisms.

DISPOSABLES
Disposable articles used for food preparation, eating, or drinking utensils, constructed wholly or in part from paper or synthetic materials and intended for one single service.

DISSOLVE
To mix a solid, dry substance with a liquid until the solid is in solution.

DIVIDER
A machine used to cut dough into a desired size or weight.

DOCKING
Punching a number of vertical impressions in a dough with a smooth round stick about the size of a pencil. Docking makes doughs expand uniformly without bursting during baking.

DOT
To place small pieces (usually butter) on the surface of food.

DOUGH
The thickened, uncooked mass of combined ingredients for bread, rolls, cookies, and pies, but usually applicable to bread.

DOUGH CONDITIONER
A chemical product added to flour to alter its properties to hold gas.

DOUGH TEMPERATURES
Temperature of dough at different stages of processing.

DRAIN
To remove liquid.

DREDGE
To sprinkle or coat with flour, sugar, or cornmeal.

DRIPPINGS
Fat and juice dripped from roasted meat.

DRY YEAST
A dehydrated form of yeast.

DU JOUR
Today's or of the day; for example, Specialite du jour — food specialty of the day.

DUSTING
Distributing a film of flour or starch on pans or work surfaces.

## E

ECLAIR
A long, thin pastry made from cream puff batter, usually filled with cream pudding, whipped topping, or ice cream. The baked, filled shell is dusted with confectioner's sugar or covered with a thin layer of chocolate.

**EDIBLE**
Fit to eat, wholesome.

**EMULSIFICATION**
The process of blending together fat and water solutions of ingredients to produce a stable mixture that will not separate while standing.

**ENCHILADAS**
A dish consisting of tortillas, a sauce, a filling (cheese, meat, or beans) and garnished with a topping such as cheese, then rolled, stacked, or folded and baked.

**ENRICHED BREAD**
Bread made from enriched flour and containing federally prescribed amounts of thiamin, riboflavin, iron, and niacin.

**ENTREE**
An intermediary course of a meal, which in the United States is usually the "main" dish.

**ENZYME**
A substance, produced by living organisms, that has the power to bring about changes in organic materials.

**EXTRACT**
Essence of fruits or spices used for flavoring.

*F*

**FAT ABSORPTION**
Fat that is absorbed in food products as they are fried in deep fat.

**FERMENTATION**
The chemical changes of an organic compound caused by action of living organisms (yeast or bacteria), usually producing a leavening gas.

**FILET**
The English term is "fillet," designating a French method of dressing fish, poultry, or meat to exclude bones and include whole muscle strips.

**FLIPPER**
A can of food that bulges at one end, indicating food spoilage. If pressed, the bulge may "flip" to the opposite end. Can and contents should be discarded.

**FOAM**
Mass of beaten egg and sugar, as in sponge cake before the flour is added.

**FOLD**
To lap yeast dough over onto itself. With cake batter, to lift and lap the batter onto itself to lightly incorporate ingredients.

## FOLD IN
To combine ingredients gently with an up-and-over motion by lifting one up through the other.

## FOOD-CONTACT SURFACES
Those parts and areas of equipment and utensils with which food normally comes in contact. Also those surfaces with which food may come in contact and drain back into surfaces normally in contact with food.

## FOOD INFECTION
A food-borne illness from ingesting foods carrying bacteria that later multiply within the body and produce disease.

## FOOD INTOXICATION
Another term used synonymously with food poisoning, or the ingestion of a food containing a poisonous substance.

## FOOD POISONING
A food-borne illness contracted through ingesting food that contains some poisonous substance.

## FOOD VALUE
The quantity of a nutrient contained in a food substance.

## FOO YOUNG
A popular dish made with scrambled eggs or omelets with cut Chinese vegetables, onions, and meat. Usually, the dish is served with a sauce.

## FORMULA
A recipe giving ingredients, amounts to be used, and the method of preparing the finished product.

## FRANCONIA POTATOES
Potatoes are parboiled, then oven-browned in butter.

## FREEZE DRYING
Drying method where the product is first frozen and then placed within a vacuum chamber (freeze dehydration). Aided by small controlled inputs of thermal or microwave energy, the moisture in the product passes directly from the ice-crystalline state to moisture vapor that is evacuated.

## FRENCH BREAD
A crusty bread, baked in a narrow strip and containing little or no shortening.

## FRENCH FRY
To cook in deep fat.

## FRICASSEE
To cook by braising; usually applied to fowl or veal cut into pieces.

**FRITTERS**
   Fruit, meat, poultry, or vegetables that are dipped in batter and fried.

**FRIZZLE**
   To cook in a small amount of fat until food is crisp and curled at the edges.

**FRY**
   To cook in hot fat. When a small amount of fat is used, the process is known as pan-frying or sauteing; when food is partially covered, shallow frying; and when food is completely covered, deep-fat frying.

**FUMIGANT**
   A gaseous or colloidal substance used to destroy insects or pests.

**FUNGICIDE**
   An agent that destroys fungi.

### G

**GARNISH**
   To ornament or decorate food before serving.

**GELATINIZE**
   To convert into a gelatinous or jelly-like form.

**GERM**
   A pathogenic, or disease-producing bacteria. A small mass of living substance capable of developing into an organism or one of its parts.

**GERMICIDE**
   A germ-destroying agent.

**GIBLETS**
   The heart, gizzard, and liver of poultry cooked with water for use in preparing chicken or turkey stock or gravy.

**GLAZE**
   A thick or thin sugar syrup or sugar mixture used to coat certain types of pastry and cakes.

**GLUTEN**
   The elastic protein mass formed when the protein material of the wheat flour is mixed with water.

**GOULASH**
   A Hungarian stew variously made in the United States of beef, veal, or frankfurters with onions and potatoes. The sauce has tomato paste and paprika as ingredients, served with sour cream if desired.

**GOURMET**
A connoisseur, or a critical judge, of good food and drink.

**GRATE**
To separate food into small pieces by rubbing it on a grater.

**GREASE**
To rub lightly with butter, shortening, or oil.

**GRIDDLE**
A flat surface or pan on which food is cooked by dry heat. Grease is removed as it accumulates. No liquid is added.

**GRILL**
See BROIL.

**GRIND**
To force food materials through a food chopper.

**GUMBO**
A Creole dish resembling soup, thickened somewhat with okra, its characteristic ingredient.

*H*

**HARD SAUCE**
A dessert sauce made of butter and confectioner's sugar, thoroughly creamed. The mixture is thinned or tempered with boiling water.

**HASH**
A baked dish made of chopped or minced meat and/or vegetables mixture in brown stock.

**HEARTH**
The heated baking surface of the floor of an oven.

**HERMITS**
A rich short-flake cookie.

**HOLLANDAISE**
A sauce made with egg yolks and butter and usually served over vegetables.

**HONEY**
A sweet syrupy substance produced by bees from flower nectar.

**HORS D'OEUVRES**
Light, snack-type foods eaten hot or cold at the beginning of a meal.

**HORSESHOES**
Danish pastry, shaped like horseshoes.

HOST
Any living animal or plant affording food for growth to a parasite.

HOT CROSS BUNS
Sweet, spicy, fruity buns with cross-cut on top, which usually is covered with a plain frosting.

HOT AIR DRYING
Products are cut in small pieces and spread on slat or wire bottom trays. Hot air is passed over and under trays to dry products.

HUMIDITY
The percent of moisture in air related to the total moisture capacity of that air at a particular temperature. Usually expressed as relative humidity.

HUNTER STYLE
Browned meat, usually chicken, braised in various combinations of tomatoes and other vegetables, stock, oil, garlic, and herbs.

HUSH PUPPIES
Deep-fried cornbread batter seasoned with onions. Used mostly in the South, usually with fish.

## *I*

INCUBATION PERIOD
That time between entrance of disease-producing bacteria in a person and the first appearance of symptoms.

INSECTICIDE
Any chemical substance used for the destruction of insects.

ITALIENNE
Italian style of cooking.

## *J*

JARDINIERE
A meat dish or garnish, "garden" style, made of several kinds of vegetables.

JULIENNE
A method of cutting meat, poultry, vegetables (especially potatoes), and fruits in long, thin strips.

## *K*

KEBAB
Various Turkish-style dishes whose principal feature is skewered meat, usually lamb.

KNEAD
　　To work and press dough with the palms of the hands, turning and folding the dough at rapid intervals.

KOLACHES
　　A bread bun made from a soft dough and topped with fruit.

## L

LACTIC ACID
　　An organic acid sometimes known as the acid of milk because it is produced when milk sours. Bacteria cause the souring.

LARDING
　　To cover uncooked lean meat or fish with strips of fat, or to insert strips of fat with a skewer.

LASAGNA
　　An Italian baked dish with broad noodles, or lasagna noodles, which has been cooked, drained, and combined in alternate layers with Italian meat sauce and cheese of two or three types (cottage, parmesan, and mozzarella).

LEAVENING
　　The aeration of a product (raising or lightening by air, steam, or gas (carbon dioxide)) that occurs during mixing and baking. The agent for generating gas in a dough or batter is usually yeast or baking powder.

LUKEWARM
　　Moderately warm or tepid.

LYONNAISE
　　A seasoning with onions originating in Lyons, France. Sauteed potatoes, green beans, and other vegetables are seasoned this way.

## M

MAKEUP
　　Manual or mechanical manipulation of dough to provide a desired size and shape.

MARBLE CAKE
　　A cake of two or three colored batters partially mixed.

MARBLING
　　The intermingling of fat with lean in meat. Meat cut across the grain will show the presence or absence of marbling and may indicate its quality and palatability.

MARINADE
　　A preparation containing spices, herbs, condiments, vegetables, and a liquid (usually acid) in which a food is placed for a period of time to enhance its flavor, or to increase its tenderness.

**MARINATE**
To cover with dressing and allow to stand for a short length of time.

**MARMALADE**
A type of jam or preserve made with sliced fruits. Crushed fruits or whole fruits are used more commonly in jam.

**MEAT SUBSTITUTE**
Any food used as an entree that does not contain beef, veal, pork, or lamb. Some substitutes are protein-rich dishes such as eggs, fish, dried beans, and cheese.

**MEDIA**
The plural of medium.

**MEDIUM**
A material or combination of materials used for cultivation of microorganisms.

**MELTING POINT**
The temperature at which a solid becomes a liquid.

**MERINGUE**
A white frothy mass of beaten egg whites and sugar.

**MILK FAT**
The fat in milk and milk products.

**MILK LIQUID**
Fresh fluid milk or evaporated or powdered milk reconstituted to the equivalent of fresh fluid milk.

**MINCE**
To cut or chop into very small pieces, using knife or chopper.

**MINESTRONE**
Thickened vegetable soup containing lentils or beans.

**MIXING**
To unite two or more ingredients.

**MOCHA**
A flavor combination of coffee and chocolate, but predominately that of coffee.

**MOLD**
Microscopic, multicellular, thread-like fungi growing on moist surfaces of organic material.

**MOLDER**
Machine that shapes dough pieces for various shapes.

**MULLIGATAWNY**
A soup with a chicken-stock base highly seasoned, chiefly by curry powder.

MYOCIDE
An agent that destroys molds.

**N**

NUTRIENT
A food substance that humans require to support life and health.

**O**

O'BRIEN
A style of preparing sauteed vegetables with diced green peppers and pimientos.

OLD DOUGHS
Overfermented yeast dough that produces a finished baked loaf, dark in crumb color, sour in flavor, low in volume, coarse in grain, and tough in texture.

OMELET
Eggs beaten to a froth, cooked with stirring until set, and served in a half-round form by folding one half over the other.

OVEN
A chamber used for baking, heating, or drying.

OYSTER MUSCLE
Tender, oval piece of dark poultry meat found in the recess on either side of the back.

**P**

PALATABLE
Agreeable to the palate or taste.

PAN BROIL
See BROIL.

PAN FRY
See FRY.

PARASITES
Organisms that live in or on a living host.

PARBOIL
To boil in water until partially cooked.

PARE
To trim and remove all superfluous matter from any article.

**PARKERHOUSE ROLLS**
Folded buns of fairly rich dough.

**PARMESAN**
A very hard, dry cheese with a sharp flavor.

**PASTA (or PASTE)**
Any macaroni product, including spaghetti, noodles, and the other pastas.

**PATHOGENS**
Disease-producing microorganisms.

**PEEL**
To remove skin, using a knife or peeling machine.

**PEPPER POT**
Any of a wide variety of styles of highly seasoned soup or stew.

**PICKLE**
A method of preserving food by a salt and water (or vinegar) solution.

**PILAF**
An oriental or Turkish dish made of rice cooked in beef or chicken stock and mildly flavored with onions.

**PIQUANT**
A tart, pleasantly sharp flavor. A piquant sauce or dressing contains lemon juice or vinegar.

**PIT**
To remove pits or seeds (as from dates or avocados).

**PLASTICITY**
The consistency or feel of shortening.

**POACH**
Method of cooking food in a hot liquid that is kept just below the boiling point.

**POLONAISE**
A garnish consisting of chopped egg and parsley served on cauliflower, asparagus, or other dishes. Bread crumbs are sometimes added.

**PPM**
Parts per million.

**PORCUPINE**
A preparation of ground beef and rice shaped into balls and cooked in tomato sauce.

**POTABLE**
Suitable for drinking.

**POTENTIALLY HAZARDOUS pH**
Any perishable food which consists in whole or in part of milk or milk products, eggs, meat, poultry, fish, shellfish, synthetic food, or other ingredient capable of supporting rapid and progressive growth of pathogens.

**PREHEAT**
To heat to the desired baking temperature before placing food in the oven.

**PROOF BOX**
A tightly closed box or cabinet equipped with shelves to permit the introduction of heat and steam; used for fermenting dough.

**PROOFING PERIOD**
The time between molding and baking during which dough rises.

**PROTOZOA**
Minute, one-celled animals.

**PROVOLONE**
A cured, hard cheese that has a smoky flavor.

**PSYCHROPHILIC BACTERIA**
Microorganisms that grow at temperatures near freezing.

**PUREE**
The pulp of a boiled food that has been rubbed through a sieve. Soup is called puree when it has been thickened with its sieved, pulpy ingredients.

## Q

**QUICK BREADS**
Bread products baked from a lean, chemically leavened batter.

## R

**RABBIT OR RAREBIT**
A melted-cheese dish.

**RAGOUT**
The French word for "stew."

**RANCID**
A disagreeable odor or flavor. Usually used to describe foods with high fat content, when oxidation occurs.

**READY-TO-COOK POULTRY**
Drawn or eviscerated poultry.

**RECONSTITUTE**
To restore the water taken from a food when it was dehydrated.

**REHYDRATE**
Combining a food with the same quantity of water that has been removed from it (see also RECONSTITUTE).

**RELISH**
A side dish, usually contrasting in color, shape, and texture to the meal. Usually designed to add flavor, zest, and interest to a meal.

**RISSOLE**
A French term meaning to obtain a crackling food by means of heat. Rissole potatoes are cooked to a golden brown crispness in fat.

**ROAST**
See BAKE.

**ROPE**
A spoiling bacterial growth in bread experienced when the dough becomes infected with bacterial spores. Poor sanitation can result in rope.

**ROUNDING OR ROUNDING UP**
Shaping of dough pieces into a ball to seal end and prevent bleeding and escape of gas.

**ROUX**
Preparation of flour and melted butter (or fat) used to thicken sauces, gravies, and soups.

**ROYAL FROSTING**
Decorative frosting of cooked sugar and egg whites.

## S

**SAFE HOLDING TEMPERATURE**
A range of cold and hot temperatures considered safe for holding potentially hazardous foods, including those refrigeration temperatures 40° F, or below, or heating temperatures 140° F, or above.

**SALISBURY STEAK**
A ground meat dish cooked with onions and made to resemble steak in shape. Sometimes referred to as hamburg steak.

**SALMONELLA INFECTION**
A type of food poisoning transmitted through foods such as poultry and poultry products containing salmonella bacteria.

**SANITIZE**
Effective bactericidal treatment of clean surfaces of equipment and utensils by an established process that is effective in destroying microorganisms.

**SAPONIFY**
To convert to soap.

**SATURATION**
> Absorption to the limit of the capacity.

**SAUERBRATEN**
> A beef pot roast cooked in a sour sauce variously prepared with spices and vinegar, and sometimes served with sour cream.

**SAUTE**
> See FRY.

**SCALD**
> To heat a liquid over hot water or direct heat to a temperature just below the boiling point.

**SCALE**
> An instrument for weighing.

**SCALING**
> Apportioning batter or dough according to unit of weight.

**SCALLOP**
> To bake food, usually cut in pieces, with a sauce or other liquid.

**SCORE**
> To cut shallow slits or gashes in the surface of food with a knife.

**SCORING**
> Judging finished goods according to points of perfection; or to cut or slash the top surface of dough pieces.

**SEASON**
> To add, or sprinkle, with seasonings or condiments.

**SHRED**
> To cut or tear into thin strips or pieces using a knife or a shredder attachment.

**SIFTING**
> Passing through fine sieve for effective blending and to remove foreign or oversize particles.

**SIMMER**
> To cook in liquid at a temperature just below the boiling point.

**SKEWER**
> A sharp metal or wood pin used to hold parts of poultry meat or skin together while being roasted.

**SKIM**
> To remove floating matter from the surface of a liquid with a spoon, ladle, or skimmer.

**SLACK DOUGH**
This is a dough that is soft and extensible but has lost its resiliency.

**SLIVER**
To cut or split into long, thin pieces.

**SMOKING**
A treatment used on most cured meat to add color and flavor.

**SMORGASBORD**
A Scandinavian-type luncheon or supper, served buffet style. Many different dishes are served, including hot and cold hors d'oeuvres, pickled vegetables, fish, assorted cheeses, jellied salads, cold and hot fish, and meats.

**SMOTHER**
To cook in a covered container, as smothered onions.

**SNAPS**
Small cookies that run flat during baking and become crisp on cooking.

**SNICKERDOODLE**
A coffeecake with a crumb topping.

**SOLIDIFYING POINT**
Temperature at which a fluid changes to a solid.

**SPORE**
Any one of various small or minute primitive reproductive bodies, capable of maintaining and reproducing itself. These are unicellular, produced by plants, molds, and bacteria.

**SPRAY DRYING**
Used for liquids and thick materials such as soup. Hot air coming into a drier contacts the small globules of the product and causes the water to be evaporated.

**SPRINGER**
A marked bulging of a food can at one or both ends. Improper exhausting of air from the can before sealing, or bacterial or chemical growth may cause swelling and spoilage.

**SPRINKLE**
To scatter in drops or small particles, such as chopped parsley, over a finished product.

**STAPHYLOCOCCI**
A family of bacteria formed in grapelike clusters, living as parasites on the outer skin and mucous membrane.

**STEAM**
To cook in steam with or without pressure.

**STEEP**
To let stand in hot liquid below boiling temperature to extract flavor, color, or other qualities from a specific food.

**STERILIZE**
To destroy microorganisms by chemical or mechanical means.

**STEW**
To simmer in liquid.

**STIR**
To blend or mix ingredients by using a spoon or other implement.

**STREPTOCOCCI**
Single-celled, globular-shaped bacteria.

**STROGANOFF**
Beef prepared with sour cream.

**STRONG FLOUR**
One that is suitable for the production of bread of good volume and quality.

**SUCCOTASH**
A combination of corn and lima beans.

**SUGAR**
To sprinkle or mix with sugar; refers to granulated unless otherwise specified in recipe.

**SUKIYAKI**
A popular Japanese dish consisting of thin slices of meat fried with onions and other vegetables, including bean sprouts, and soy sauce containing seasoning, herbs, and spices.

**SWELLER**
A can of food having both ends bulging as a result of spoilage. Swellers should be discarded, except molasses, in which this condition is normal in a warm climate.

*T*

**TABLEWARE**
A general term referring to multi use eating and drinking utensils, including knives, forks, spoons, and dishes.

**TACO**
An open-face sandwich, Mexican style, made of fried tortillas shaped like a shell and filled with a hot meat-vegetable mixture.

**TAMALE**
A highly seasoned steamed dish made of cornmeal with ground beef or chicken rolled in the center.

**TARTAR**
A rich sauce made with salad dressing, onions, parsley, and sometimes pickle relish, olives, and cucumbers, served with fish and shellfish.

**TARTS**
Small pastries with heavy fruit or cream filling.

**TEMPERING**
Adjusting temperature of ingredients to a certain degree.

**TETRAZINNI**
An Italian dish with chicken, green peppers, and onions mixed in spaghetti and served with shredded cheese.

**TEXTURE**
The quality of the interior structure of a baked product. Usually sensed by the touch of the cut surface as well as by sight and taste.

**THERMOSTAT**
A device for maintaining constant temperature.

**THICKEN**
To transform a thin liquid into a thick one either by the gelatinization of flour starches or the coagulation of egg protein.

**TOAST**
To brown the surface of a food by the application of direct heat.

**TORTILLA**
A Mexican bread made with white corn flour and water. Special techniques are used in handling the dough to roll it thin as a pie crust. It is baked on an ungreased griddle or in the oven.

**TOSS**
To lightly mix one or more ingredients. Usually refers to salad ingredients.

**TOXIN**
A waste product, given off by an organism causing contamination of food and subsequent illness in human beings. It is the toxin of a disease-producing germ that causes the poisoning.

**TRICHINOSIS**
A food-borne disease transmitted through pork containing a parasite, Trichinella spirallis, or its larvae, which infects animals.

**TROUGHS**
Large containers, usually on wheels, used for holding large masses of raising dough.

**TRUSS**
To bind or fasten together the wings and legs of poultry with the aid of string or metal skewers.

23

## V

### VACUUM DRYING
Vacuum is applied to liquids and fills the liquid with bubbles, creating a puffing effect. The puffed product is then dried, leaving a solid fragile mass. This is then crushed to reduce bulk.

### VERMICELLI
A pasta, slightly yellow in color, shaped like spaghetti and very thin.

### VINAIGRETTE
A mixture of oil and vinegar seasoned with salt, pepper, and herbs, used in sauces and dressings.

### VIRUS
A group of organisms of ultramicroscopic size that grow in living tissue and may produce disease in animals and plants. Viruses are smaller than bacteria and, hence, pass through membranes or filters.

## W

### WASH
A liquid brushed on the surface of an unbaked or baked product (may be water, milk, starch solution, thin syrup, or egg).

### WATER ABSORPTION
Water required to produce a bread dough of desired consistency. Flours vary in ability to absorb water, depending on the age of the flour, moisture content, wheat from which it is milled, storage conditions, and milling process.

### WHEY
Liquid remaining after the removal of fat, casein, and other substances from milk.

### WHIP
To beat rapidly to increase volume by incorporating air.

## Y

### YEAST
A group of small, single-celled plants, oval in shape and several times larger than bacteria. Yeast helps to promote fermentation and is useful in producing bread, cheese, wine, and so on.

### YOUNG DOUGHS
Underfermented yeast dough producing finished yeast goods that are light in color, tight in grain, and low in volume (heavy).

## Z

### ZWIEBACK
A toast made of bread or plain coffeecake dried in slow oven.

# ANSWER SHEET

TEST NO. _____ PART _____ TITLE OF POSITION _____
(AS GIVEN IN EXAMINATION ANNOUNCEMENT - INCLUDE OPTION, IF ANY)

PLACE OF EXAMINATION _____ DATE_____
(CITY OR TOWN)                          (STATE)

RATING

---

## USE THE SPECIAL PENCIL.    MAKE GLOSSY BLACK MARKS.

| # | A B C D E | # | A B C D E | # | A B C D E | # | A B C D E | # | A B C D E |
|---|---|---|---|---|---|---|---|---|---|
| 1 | ‖ ‖ ‖ ‖ ‖ | 26 | ‖ ‖ ‖ ‖ ‖ | 51 | ‖ ‖ ‖ ‖ ‖ | 76 | ‖ ‖ ‖ ‖ ‖ | 101 | ‖ ‖ ‖ ‖ ‖ |
| 2 | ‖ ‖ ‖ ‖ ‖ | 27 | ‖ ‖ ‖ ‖ ‖ | 52 | ‖ ‖ ‖ ‖ ‖ | 77 | ‖ ‖ ‖ ‖ ‖ | 102 | ‖ ‖ ‖ ‖ ‖ |
| 3 | ‖ ‖ ‖ ‖ ‖ | 28 | ‖ ‖ ‖ ‖ ‖ | 53 | ‖ ‖ ‖ ‖ ‖ | 78 | ‖ ‖ ‖ ‖ ‖ | 103 | ‖ ‖ ‖ ‖ ‖ |
| 4 | ‖ ‖ ‖ ‖ ‖ | 29 | ‖ ‖ ‖ ‖ ‖ | 54 | ‖ ‖ ‖ ‖ ‖ | 79 | ‖ ‖ ‖ ‖ ‖ | 104 | ‖ ‖ ‖ ‖ ‖ |
| 5 | ‖ ‖ ‖ ‖ ‖ | 30 | ‖ ‖ ‖ ‖ ‖ | 55 | ‖ ‖ ‖ ‖ ‖ | 80 | ‖ ‖ ‖ ‖ ‖ | 105 | ‖ ‖ ‖ ‖ ‖ |
| 6 | ‖ ‖ ‖ ‖ ‖ | 31 | ‖ ‖ ‖ ‖ ‖ | 56 | ‖ ‖ ‖ ‖ ‖ | 81 | ‖ ‖ ‖ ‖ ‖ | 106 | ‖ ‖ ‖ ‖ ‖ |
| 7 | ‖ ‖ ‖ ‖ ‖ | 32 | ‖ ‖ ‖ ‖ ‖ | 57 | ‖ ‖ ‖ ‖ ‖ | 82 | ‖ ‖ ‖ ‖ ‖ | 107 | ‖ ‖ ‖ ‖ ‖ |
| 8 | ‖ ‖ ‖ ‖ ‖ | 33 | ‖ ‖ ‖ ‖ ‖ | 58 | ‖ ‖ ‖ ‖ ‖ | 83 | ‖ ‖ ‖ ‖ ‖ | 108 | ‖ ‖ ‖ ‖ ‖ |
| 9 | ‖ ‖ ‖ ‖ ‖ | 34 | ‖ ‖ ‖ ‖ ‖ | 59 | ‖ ‖ ‖ ‖ ‖ | 84 | ‖ ‖ ‖ ‖ ‖ | 109 | ‖ ‖ ‖ ‖ ‖ |
| 10 | ‖ ‖ ‖ ‖ ‖ | 35 | ‖ ‖ ‖ ‖ ‖ | 60 | ‖ ‖ ‖ ‖ ‖ | 85 | ‖ ‖ ‖ ‖ ‖ | 110 | ‖ ‖ ‖ ‖ ‖ |

Make only ONE mark for each answer.   Additional and stray marks may be
counted as mistakes.   In making corrections, erase errors COMPLETELY.

| # | A B C D E | # | A B C D E | # | A B C D E | # | A B C D E | # | A B C D E |
|---|---|---|---|---|---|---|---|---|---|
| 11 | ‖ ‖ ‖ ‖ ‖ | 36 | ‖ ‖ ‖ ‖ ‖ | 61 | ‖ ‖ ‖ ‖ ‖ | 86 | ‖ ‖ ‖ ‖ ‖ | 111 | ‖ ‖ ‖ ‖ ‖ |
| 12 | ‖ ‖ ‖ ‖ ‖ | 37 | ‖ ‖ ‖ ‖ ‖ | 62 | ‖ ‖ ‖ ‖ ‖ | 87 | ‖ ‖ ‖ ‖ ‖ | 112 | ‖ ‖ ‖ ‖ ‖ |
| 13 | ‖ ‖ ‖ ‖ ‖ | 38 | ‖ ‖ ‖ ‖ ‖ | 63 | ‖ ‖ ‖ ‖ ‖ | 88 | ‖ ‖ ‖ ‖ ‖ | 113 | ‖ ‖ ‖ ‖ ‖ |
| 14 | ‖ ‖ ‖ ‖ ‖ | 39 | ‖ ‖ ‖ ‖ ‖ | 64 | ‖ ‖ ‖ ‖ ‖ | 89 | ‖ ‖ ‖ ‖ ‖ | 114 | ‖ ‖ ‖ ‖ ‖ |
| 15 | ‖ ‖ ‖ ‖ ‖ | 40 | ‖ ‖ ‖ ‖ ‖ | 65 | ‖ ‖ ‖ ‖ ‖ | 90 | ‖ ‖ ‖ ‖ ‖ | 115 | ‖ ‖ ‖ ‖ ‖ |
| 16 | ‖ ‖ ‖ ‖ ‖ | 41 | ‖ ‖ ‖ ‖ ‖ | 66 | ‖ ‖ ‖ ‖ ‖ | 91 | ‖ ‖ ‖ ‖ ‖ | 116 | ‖ ‖ ‖ ‖ ‖ |
| 17 | ‖ ‖ ‖ ‖ ‖ | 42 | ‖ ‖ ‖ ‖ ‖ | 67 | ‖ ‖ ‖ ‖ ‖ | 92 | ‖ ‖ ‖ ‖ ‖ | 117 | ‖ ‖ ‖ ‖ ‖ |
| 18 | ‖ ‖ ‖ ‖ ‖ | 43 | ‖ ‖ ‖ ‖ ‖ | 68 | ‖ ‖ ‖ ‖ ‖ | 93 | ‖ ‖ ‖ ‖ ‖ | 118 | ‖ ‖ ‖ ‖ ‖ |
| 19 | ‖ ‖ ‖ ‖ ‖ | 44 | ‖ ‖ ‖ ‖ ‖ | 69 | ‖ ‖ ‖ ‖ ‖ | 94 | ‖ ‖ ‖ ‖ ‖ | 119 | ‖ ‖ ‖ ‖ ‖ |
| 20 | ‖ ‖ ‖ ‖ ‖ | 45 | ‖ ‖ ‖ ‖ ‖ | 70 | ‖ ‖ ‖ ‖ ‖ | 95 | ‖ ‖ ‖ ‖ ‖ | 120 | ‖ ‖ ‖ ‖ ‖ |
| 21 | ‖ ‖ ‖ ‖ ‖ | 46 | ‖ ‖ ‖ ‖ ‖ | 71 | ‖ ‖ ‖ ‖ ‖ | 96 | ‖ ‖ ‖ ‖ ‖ | 121 | ‖ ‖ ‖ ‖ ‖ |
| 22 | ‖ ‖ ‖ ‖ ‖ | 47 | ‖ ‖ ‖ ‖ ‖ | 72 | ‖ ‖ ‖ ‖ ‖ | 97 | ‖ ‖ ‖ ‖ ‖ | 122 | ‖ ‖ ‖ ‖ ‖ |
| 23 | ‖ ‖ ‖ ‖ ‖ | 48 | ‖ ‖ ‖ ‖ ‖ | 73 | ‖ ‖ ‖ ‖ ‖ | 98 | ‖ ‖ ‖ ‖ ‖ | 123 | ‖ ‖ ‖ ‖ ‖ |
| 24 | ‖ ‖ ‖ ‖ ‖ | 49 | ‖ ‖ ‖ ‖ ‖ | 74 | ‖ ‖ ‖ ‖ ‖ | 99 | ‖ ‖ ‖ ‖ ‖ | 124 | ‖ ‖ ‖ ‖ ‖ |
| 25 | ‖ ‖ ‖ ‖ ‖ | 50 | ‖ ‖ ‖ ‖ ‖ | 75 | ‖ ‖ ‖ ‖ ‖ | 100 | ‖ ‖ ‖ ‖ ‖ | 125 | ‖ ‖ ‖ ‖ ‖ |

# ANSWER SHEET

TEST NO. _____ PART _____ TITLE OF POSITION _____

(AS GIVEN IN EXAMINATION ANNOUNCEMENT - INCLUDE OPTION, IF ANY)

PLACE OF EXAMINATION _____ DATE_____

(CITY OR TOWN)　　　　　　　　　　　(STATE)

RATING

---

## USE THE SPECIAL PENCIL.　MAKE GLOSSY BLACK MARKS.

|   | A B C D E |   | A B C D E |   | A B C D E |   | A B C D E |   | A B C D E |
|---|---|---|---|---|---|---|---|---|---|
| 1 | ⁞ ⁞ ⁞ ⁞ ⁞ | 26 | ⁞ ⁞ ⁞ ⁞ ⁞ | 51 | ⁞ ⁞ ⁞ ⁞ ⁞ | 76 | ⁞ ⁞ ⁞ ⁞ ⁞ | 101 | ⁞ ⁞ ⁞ ⁞ ⁞ |
| 2 | ⁞ ⁞ ⁞ ⁞ ⁞ | 27 | ⁞ ⁞ ⁞ ⁞ ⁞ | 52 | ⁞ ⁞ ⁞ ⁞ ⁞ | 77 | ⁞ ⁞ ⁞ ⁞ ⁞ | 102 | ⁞ ⁞ ⁞ ⁞ ⁞ |
| 3 | ⁞ ⁞ ⁞ ⁞ ⁞ | 28 | ⁞ ⁞ ⁞ ⁞ ⁞ | 53 | ⁞ ⁞ ⁞ ⁞ ⁞ | 78 | ⁞ ⁞ ⁞ ⁞ ⁞ | 103 | ⁞ ⁞ ⁞ ⁞ ⁞ |
| 4 | ⁞ ⁞ ⁞ ⁞ ⁞ | 29 | ⁞ ⁞ ⁞ ⁞ ⁞ | 54 | ⁞ ⁞ ⁞ ⁞ ⁞ | 79 | ⁞ ⁞ ⁞ ⁞ ⁞ | 104 | ⁞ ⁞ ⁞ ⁞ ⁞ |
| 5 | ⁞ ⁞ ⁞ ⁞ ⁞ | 30 | ⁞ ⁞ ⁞ ⁞ ⁞ | 55 | ⁞ ⁞ ⁞ ⁞ ⁞ | 80 | ⁞ ⁞ ⁞ ⁞ ⁞ | 105 | ⁞ ⁞ ⁞ ⁞ ⁞ |
| 6 | ⁞ ⁞ ⁞ ⁞ ⁞ | 31 | ⁞ ⁞ ⁞ ⁞ ⁞ | 56 | ⁞ ⁞ ⁞ ⁞ ⁞ | 81 | ⁞ ⁞ ⁞ ⁞ ⁞ | 106 | ⁞ ⁞ ⁞ ⁞ ⁞ |
| 7 | ⁞ ⁞ ⁞ ⁞ ⁞ | 32 | ⁞ ⁞ ⁞ ⁞ ⁞ | 57 | ⁞ ⁞ ⁞ ⁞ ⁞ | 82 | ⁞ ⁞ ⁞ ⁞ ⁞ | 107 | ⁞ ⁞ ⁞ ⁞ ⁞ |
| 8 | ⁞ ⁞ ⁞ ⁞ ⁞ | 33 | ⁞ ⁞ ⁞ ⁞ ⁞ | 58 | ⁞ ⁞ ⁞ ⁞ ⁞ | 83 | ⁞ ⁞ ⁞ ⁞ ⁞ | 108 | ⁞ ⁞ ⁞ ⁞ ⁞ |
| 9 | ⁞ ⁞ ⁞ ⁞ ⁞ | 34 | ⁞ ⁞ ⁞ ⁞ ⁞ | 59 | ⁞ ⁞ ⁞ ⁞ ⁞ | 84 | ⁞ ⁞ ⁞ ⁞ ⁞ | 109 | ⁞ ⁞ ⁞ ⁞ ⁞ |
| 10 | ⁞ ⁞ ⁞ ⁞ ⁞ | 35 | ⁞ ⁞ ⁞ ⁞ ⁞ | 60 | ⁞ ⁞ ⁞ ⁞ ⁞ | 85 | ⁞ ⁞ ⁞ ⁞ ⁞ | 110 | ⁞ ⁞ ⁞ ⁞ ⁞ |

Make only ONE mark for each answer.　Additional and stray marks may be
counted as mistakes.　In making corrections, erase errors COMPLETELY.

|   | A B C D E |   | A B C D E |   | A B C D E |   | A B C D E |   | A B C D E |
|---|---|---|---|---|---|---|---|---|---|
| 11 | ⁞ ⁞ ⁞ ⁞ ⁞ | 36 | ⁞ ⁞ ⁞ ⁞ ⁞ | 61 | ⁞ ⁞ ⁞ ⁞ ⁞ | 86 | ⁞ ⁞ ⁞ ⁞ ⁞ | 111 | ⁞ ⁞ ⁞ ⁞ ⁞ |
| 12 | ⁞ ⁞ ⁞ ⁞ ⁞ | 37 | ⁞ ⁞ ⁞ ⁞ ⁞ | 62 | ⁞ ⁞ ⁞ ⁞ ⁞ | 87 | ⁞ ⁞ ⁞ ⁞ ⁞ | 112 | ⁞ ⁞ ⁞ ⁞ ⁞ |
| 13 | ⁞ ⁞ ⁞ ⁞ ⁞ | 38 | ⁞ ⁞ ⁞ ⁞ ⁞ | 63 | ⁞ ⁞ ⁞ ⁞ ⁞ | 88 | ⁞ ⁞ ⁞ ⁞ ⁞ | 113 | ⁞ ⁞ ⁞ ⁞ ⁞ |
| 14 | ⁞ ⁞ ⁞ ⁞ ⁞ | 39 | ⁞ ⁞ ⁞ ⁞ ⁞ | 64 | ⁞ ⁞ ⁞ ⁞ ⁞ | 89 | ⁞ ⁞ ⁞ ⁞ ⁞ | 114 | ⁞ ⁞ ⁞ ⁞ ⁞ |
| 15 | ⁞ ⁞ ⁞ ⁞ ⁞ | 40 | ⁞ ⁞ ⁞ ⁞ ⁞ | 65 | ⁞ ⁞ ⁞ ⁞ ⁞ | 90 | ⁞ ⁞ ⁞ ⁞ ⁞ | 115 | ⁞ ⁞ ⁞ ⁞ ⁞ |
| 16 | ⁞ ⁞ ⁞ ⁞ ⁞ | 41 | ⁞ ⁞ ⁞ ⁞ ⁞ | 66 | ⁞ ⁞ ⁞ ⁞ ⁞ | 91 | ⁞ ⁞ ⁞ ⁞ ⁞ | 116 | ⁞ ⁞ ⁞ ⁞ ⁞ |
| 17 | ⁞ ⁞ ⁞ ⁞ ⁞ | 42 | ⁞ ⁞ ⁞ ⁞ ⁞ | 67 | ⁞ ⁞ ⁞ ⁞ ⁞ | 92 | ⁞ ⁞ ⁞ ⁞ ⁞ | 117 | ⁞ ⁞ ⁞ ⁞ ⁞ |
| 18 | ⁞ ⁞ ⁞ ⁞ ⁞ | 43 | ⁞ ⁞ ⁞ ⁞ ⁞ | 68 | ⁞ ⁞ ⁞ ⁞ ⁞ | 93 | ⁞ ⁞ ⁞ ⁞ ⁞ | 118 | ⁞ ⁞ ⁞ ⁞ ⁞ |
| 19 | ⁞ ⁞ ⁞ ⁞ ⁞ | 44 | ⁞ ⁞ ⁞ ⁞ ⁞ | 69 | ⁞ ⁞ ⁞ ⁞ ⁞ | 94 | ⁞ ⁞ ⁞ ⁞ ⁞ | 119 | ⁞ ⁞ ⁞ ⁞ ⁞ |
| 20 | ⁞ ⁞ ⁞ ⁞ ⁞ | 45 | ⁞ ⁞ ⁞ ⁞ ⁞ | 70 | ⁞ ⁞ ⁞ ⁞ ⁞ | 95 | ⁞ ⁞ ⁞ ⁞ ⁞ | 120 | ⁞ ⁞ ⁞ ⁞ ⁞ |
| 21 | ⁞ ⁞ ⁞ ⁞ ⁞ | 46 | ⁞ ⁞ ⁞ ⁞ ⁞ | 71 | ⁞ ⁞ ⁞ ⁞ ⁞ | 96 | ⁞ ⁞ ⁞ ⁞ ⁞ | 121 | ⁞ ⁞ ⁞ ⁞ ⁞ |
| 22 | ⁞ ⁞ ⁞ ⁞ ⁞ | 47 | ⁞ ⁞ ⁞ ⁞ ⁞ | 72 | ⁞ ⁞ ⁞ ⁞ ⁞ | 97 | ⁞ ⁞ ⁞ ⁞ ⁞ | 122 | ⁞ ⁞ ⁞ ⁞ ⁞ |
| 23 | ⁞ ⁞ ⁞ ⁞ ⁞ | 48 | ⁞ ⁞ ⁞ ⁞ ⁞ | 73 | ⁞ ⁞ ⁞ ⁞ ⁞ | 98 | ⁞ ⁞ ⁞ ⁞ ⁞ | 123 | ⁞ ⁞ ⁞ ⁞ ⁞ |
| 24 | ⁞ ⁞ ⁞ ⁞ ⁞ | 49 | ⁞ ⁞ ⁞ ⁞ ⁞ | 74 | ⁞ ⁞ ⁞ ⁞ ⁞ | 99 | ⁞ ⁞ ⁞ ⁞ ⁞ | 124 | ⁞ ⁞ ⁞ ⁞ ⁞ |
| 25 | ⁞ ⁞ ⁞ ⁞ ⁞ | 50 | ⁞ ⁞ ⁞ ⁞ ⁞ | 75 | ⁞ ⁞ ⁞ ⁞ ⁞ | 100 | ⁞ ⁞ ⁞ ⁞ ⁞ | 125 | ⁞ ⁞ ⁞ ⁞ ⁞ |